BRITAIN IN OLD PHOTOGRAPHS

PALACE PIER, BRIGHTON

ALBERT BULLOCK &
PETER MEDCALF

SUTTON PUBLISHING LIMITED

Sutton Publishing Limited
Phoenix Mill · Thrupp · Stroud
Gloucestershire · GL5 2BU

First published 1999

Copyright © Albert Bullock &
  Peter Medcalf, 1999

Title page: The Palace Pier, 1997

British Library Cataloguing in Publication Data
A catalogue record for this book is available from the
British Library.

ISBN 0-7509-1974-4

Typeset in 10/12 Perpetua.
Typesetting and origination by
Sutton Publishing Limited.
Printed in Great Britain by
Ebenezer Baylis, Worcester.

Edwardian view towards Volk's Electric Railway, situated to the east of the Palace Pier. The promenade looks busy, with the 4*d* return fare to Black Rock to view the *Daily Mail* waterplanes proving extremely popular. On the beach, souvenirs are being offered to tempt the day-trippers.

CONTENTS

Charabanc tour outside the Palace Pier, *c.* 1919. There are two soldiers sitting with their backs to the sea. 'History with its flickering lamp stumbles along the trail of the past, trying to reconstruct its scenes to revive its echoes and kindle with pale gleams the passion of former days.' (Winston Churchill, House of Commons, 12 November 1940)

FOREWORD

O f Britain's forty-three extant Victorian and Edwardian piers, half are in private
hands but no more than seventeen survive in anything like their original form.
Included within both these statistics is Brighton's Palace Pier which has been
the scene of promenading and other typically pier activities and entertainments since its
official opening by the Mayoress of Brighton on 20 May 1899. A centenary story rightly
deserves celebration and this has been well executed by Albert Bullock and Peter
Medcalf, for whom the subject of piers encompasses a great deal of social, economic
and local history, in addition to the development of art, engineering and shipping. All
these and other aspects have been carefully researched and analysed. A fascinating and
readable text is strongly supported by no fewer than 235 illustrations, which are
remarkable both for their origin and variety. I have much pleasure in commending to
you *The Palace Pier, Brighton.*

Dr John Whyman

Brighton Beach with West Battery and Battery House, *c.* 1795. This painting by Richard Earlom
(1743–1822) (pen, ink, pencil, watercolour and body colour 22.8 × 28 cm) shows Brighton fishermen
drawing in the hog-boats, which weighed 8–12 tons, during a rough sea. A fashionably dressed lady and
gentleman saunter along the beach with their dog. In the middle distance the bathing machines indicate
that 'taking a dip' was well established.

INTRODUCTION

The Sussex Coastal Plain which lies between the South Downs and the English Channel had for generations been inhabited by communities who made their living by farming and fishing. The community of Brighthelmstone, which successfully fished in nearby waters and the North Sea, was about 3,000 strong by the end of the seventeenth century. It was probably because the inhabitants dragged their boats on to the sheltered beach further west and had no man-made harbour that a myth later arose that the place was of no consequence until its 'discovery' by the medical profession and aristocracy during the eighteenth century. Nevertheless, when Dr Richard Russell's Latin treatise was translated into English in 1752, under the title *A Dissertation on the use of Seawater in Diseases of the Glands*, Brighthelmstone was near enough to London and the Court to benefit from the latest medical fashion and to start the slow erosion of Bath's monopoly as the nation's premier resort. Like Bath the reputation of Brighthelmstone, or Brighton as it became abbreviated, was as a health resort which shortly gave way to that of a leisure resort where the aristocracy and the wealthy landed gentry could take part in the fashionable pastimes of the day. The exclusivity of the resort was maintained as the only practical way of reaching it was by road and, although improved with lighter and more comfortable coaches and the use of turnpike-trusts to repair the roads, it was still an expensive journey. Under favourable weather conditions boats could arrive at Margate within a few hours, but the longer voyage to Brighton put her beyond the reach of all except the very wealthy who could afford the overland journey.

The patronage of the Prince of Wales and his circle from 1783 ensured Brighton's success and the town was extended well beyond The Lanes, a seventeenth-century district of narrow, twisting lanes lined with fishermen's cottages. Appropriately the dominant architectural style was 'Regency' which mirrored John Nash's development of the West End of the capital. The Royal Crescent, Regency Square and Clifton Terrace epitomized this style and expressed the town's growing confidence as the heir to Bath. The Royal Pavilion, the residence of the Prince of Wales since 1787, was redesigned by Nash in 1815 in the outrageous manner of an Indian mogul's palace crowned with onion-shaped domes and tent-like roofs, while the interior was lavishly decorated in the Chinese fashion. It was this building more than any other that set the tone of the town and determined the behaviour of its visitors. Rapid growth took place and its 1801 population of about 7,000 had increased to more than 24,000, twenty years later, by which time the town had grown westwards to Hove and eastwards in the form of Kemp Town.

Communications, however, were to improve and the arrival of the railway in the 1840s widened the social scale of visitors from the capital and made the town less exclusive. Brighton came within the reach of both those on salaries and, eventually, weekly paid workers after the passing of the Bank Holiday Act (1871). The railway companies were not slow to learn how to profit from cheap excursion trains for weekend and daily visitors. Standards of living were rising for all but the poorest Londoners during the last decades of the nineteenth century and Brighton, far from resisting new visitors, also learnt to profit from them. Popular entertainments such as music halls, fun-fairs, public bands and public houses gave Brighton an air of brashness that had been typical of Margate for many years. Some of its aristocratic atmosphere was retained, although Queen Victoria disliked the place and refused to reside there, but its name was soon to become synonymous with the fancies and pleasures of people who were temporarily away from the watchful eyes of their moral guardians and neighbours.

A

DISSERTATION

On the U S E of

SEA-WATER

IN THE

DISEASES of the GLANDS.

PARTICULARLY

The *Scurvy, Jaundice, King's-Evil, Le-profy,* and the *Glandular Confumption.*

Tranflated from the *Latin* of

R I C H A R D   R U S S E L, M. D.

The T H I R D E D I T I O N, Revifed and Corrected.

To which is added,

A COMMENTARY on SEA-WATER,

Tranflated from the *Latin* of

J. S P E E D, M. D.

Both by an EMINENT PHYSICIAN.

L O N D O N:

Printed for W. OWEN, at *Homer's* Head, *Temple-Bar.*

MDCCLV.

The treatment with sea-water was split into two parts: firstly swimming in the sea with the water as cold as possible, and secondly, drinking sea water. Hot sea water could be mixed with a concoction of milk, crab's cream of tartar, prepared woodlice and viper's skin. The King's Evil mentioned on the title page (left) relates to diseases of the skin. It was thought at one point that this was curable by the king's (or queen's) touch. This practice started with Edward the Confessor and continued up to the death of Queen Anne in 1714.

'Doctor Brighton'. Dr Richard Russell (1687–1759) of Lewes could be called the father of modern Brighton. He came from a medical background, his father being a surgeon and apothecary. His ideas about the use of sea water were based on ancient Greek medical writings. Many of his ideas were very advanced, notably the value of fresh air, and his treatment was a balance between diet and hygiene. He was described by the poet Michelet in 1861 as 'L'inventeur de la mer'. This portrait by Benjamin Wilson (1721–88) hangs in the Royal Pavilion. Wilson, who was born in Leeds, was also an etcher and scientist. He was considered one of the leading portrait painters in England during the 1750s. He went on to paint theatrical pieces including David Garrick as Hamlet and King Lear.

The Prince Regent entering a bathing machine at Brighton in 1818. As Prince of Wales he first visited Brighton in 1783 for a short stay. In 1784 there followed a longer visit at which he took a course of sea bathing for glandular trouble. It is at this point that what has been described as one of the most 'remarkable chapters in the history of the English seaside had opened. Where Royalty ventured servants went – shopkeepers followed – hoteliers and the whole great spectacle of pleasure and profit.'

Photographic postcard of the Royal Pavilion, 1910. Queen Victoria and Prince Albert disliked the Royal Pavilion, finding the residents of Brighton 'indiscreet and troublesome'. After her last visit to Brighton in 1845 the Pavilion was closed; it was sold by the Crown to the townspeople in 1847 at a cost of £50,000. The original building price must have been near to half a million pounds. The Queen purchased Osborne House on the Isle of Wight in September of 1846 and this became her marine palace far away from the public gaze of day-trippers.

CHAPTER ONE

BRIGHTON'S EARLIER PIERS

The Palace Pier was preceded by the Chain Pier, which had been opened in 1823, and by the West Pier that followed in 1866. The purpose of the Chain Pier had been to meet the requirements of a growing number of passenger ships from the French port of Dieppe. These ships had relied upon rowing boats, locally known as 'punts', to ferry passengers ashore and to drag rafts behind them upon which baggage, horses and carriages were conveyed. Passenger comfort and the dignity of Brighton led to a growing demand for the construction of a pier upon which disembarkation could take place. The Suspension Chain Pier, or the Old Chain Pier as it came to be known, survived until 1896 when it was destroyed by a storm. Its owners were not slow to recognize its commercial value beyond its use as a landing stage for boats. Additional revenue could be raised by charging promenaders an entry fee of 2d. Shops were erected along its 1,134-ft length and visitors were entertained by a 'camera obscura', a windowless room with a small aperture through which a panoramic view of the sea-front was projected. Kiosks were also built to accommodate the sale of souvenirs and confectionery, and a fortune-teller. These additional commercial ventures set a precedent of which later pier builders took account. As a favourite subject for nineteenth-century artists, including J.M.W. Turner, images of the Chain Pier travelled far and wide as paintings, engravings and on souvenir pottery.

Brighton's West Pier represented a more elaborate design and was built when investors were well aware of the importance of attracting visitors throughout the year. The West Pier's designer, Eugenius Birch, found his inspiration in the oriental grandeur of the Royal Pavilion, and his masterpiece aptly included a pavilion that was later used as a theatre.

By the late nineteenth century the Chain Pier's state of disrepair and the growing success of Brighton as a resort raised the question of its replacement. In 1886 The Palace Pier Company was formed for this purpose and received parliamentary approval by the Brighton Marine Palace and Pier Act (1888) for raising the capital sum of £150,000 by subscription. The cost of the Chain Pier's demolition was to be covered by this sum.

Chain Pier showing the original esplanade which was 1,248 ft long, 1823. Engineer Ralph Dodd proposed on 9 December 1819 that a company should be formed to build a 'sea jetty or water promenade'. Shares were offered at £100 each and a total of £27,000 was raised to form the Brighton Pier Co. in 1821. Captain Samuel Brown, a naval architect and marine engineer, was appointed as engineer. He was responsible for the introduction of chain cables to the Royal Navy and owned a chain manufacturing company in London. The pier was built using the same principle as he had used at Leith Pier in Scotland in 1821, re-adapting the suspension bridge design. The contract was awarded to M. MacIntosh and work commenced on 11 September 1822. The foundation consisted of four clusters of seventy piles of Norwegian firs which were thickly covered in pitch. The piles were metal pointed for better penetration into the chalk. The anticipated yearly revenue from the pier was £8,000, of which £2,500 was to be derived from payments of 2s a head from 25,000 passengers using steam packets, and the balance from promenaders. These estimates were never reached. Clearly visible on the extreme left-hand side of this drawing is the treadmill which was worked by donkeys to raise water for street cleaning. There is a fine view of Marine Parade with its Regency front.

Compliments from Brighton. This postcard was posted on February 1903. It shows the Chain Pier with the unfinished Palace Pier. The view dates from 1895.

Opposite: On the Chain Pier, Brighton, from an illustration in an 1862 guide to Brighton. Stalls sold silhouette portraits, souvenir china, prints and wax flowers. There was a reading-room and a camera obscura. The latter was first described by Leonardo da Vinci in 1515, and the artist Canaletto (1697–1768) used one as an aid to his painting in Venice. During 1861 6*d* was charged for admission to the camera obscura, the view being of the coast from Newhaven to Worthing. Ellen Terry's wine shop was licensed for wine and tobacco; the cherry brandy was highly recommended.

The Chain Pier was run by a joint stock company incorporated by an Act of Parliament dated 5 July 1822 as the above dividend receipt shows. The annual ticket of admission (top left and right) could only be used by family and servants and not by visitors.

Chain Pier front entrance, *c.* 1870. A poster advertises 'Bathing'. The pier had been visited by many distinguished people over the years including British and foreign royalty. William IV enjoyed promenading on the Chain Pier, where he would distribute sweets to children as he took the sea air.

This photograph was taken from a Victorian lantern slide, *c.* 1880. Although the Chain Pier was 1,134 ft long, it was only 13 ft wide with neat cast-iron railings. When the West Pier opened in 1866 and the aquarium in 1871 the Chain Pier lost its exclusivity and its fortunes changed. The rise of Newhaven as a cross-Channel port had an adverse effect on the revenue from the steampacket trade.

The Old Chain Pier, Brighton, *c.* 1893, a painting in grisaille ink and wash (34.5 × 24 cm). This naive study by an amateur artist, Arthur Elliot, shows fishermen using the lower deck. It was painted as part of a series during the period 1892–4. Obviously this was a popular spot for local fishermen.

A George Ruff photograph, probably taken from the West Pier, 1896. Trousers rolled up, the children are enjoying a jolly good paddle! In the distance is the half-completed structure of the Palace Pier, with the Chain Pier behind. Brighton-based photographer George Ruff Jnr was born in 1858 and died at the end of the Edwardian era. His father, a professional photographer, had set up business in the mid-1850s with a studio at 45 Queens Road, Brighton. Ruff Jnr worked through the early days of the 'snap shot', using a hand-held camera, and captured scenes from daily life in the town.

A fine view of the Chain Pier entrance and along the deck, *c.* 1896. Bathing is advertised at the pier head and the town band is billed to perform on Sundays at 11.30 a.m. and 3.30 p.m. The photograph shows the chain cable which was embedded into the cliff behind.

View from the Old Chain Pier head looking towards the coast, *c*. 1896. On the extreme left are two amusement machines produced by the Mechanical Trading Co. – 'Try your Grip' and 'Try your Twist' – both designed to test one's strength and each costing a penny a go.

The beach is busy at low tide to the east of the Royal Chain Pier, c. 1896. This is another George Ruff photograph. Families are enjoying picnics and promenaders are silhouetted as they saunter along the Chain Pier.

When the West Pier – designed by Eugenius Birch, the doyen of pier engineers – was completed in October 1866, its beauty was much admired by the 1,600 visitors who passed through the turnstiles on its first day. It cost £30,000 and the original share capital was £25,000. At first it was a simple but elegant wooden and iron promenade with a few kiosks. It was extended during 1893 with a southern end pavilion, bandstand, glass windshield and shelters. At the pier head landing stages were added to accommodate paddle-steamers and swimmers. In 1916 a concert hall was completed. The large ornate theatre, initially called the New Pavilion, had 1,400 seats. Before the First World War a young Charlie Chaplin and Stan Laurel appeared there in 'Casey's Court', a knockabout music-hall show, from which they later found fame in America.

Postcard looking along Grand Junction Road leading into Kings Road (named after George IV), with not a motor car in sight, 1905. The area between the piers was used by local fishermen, whose nets can be seen laid out on the beach. 'All Aboard the *Skylark*' – the boat with sails up looks as if it is preparing to take visitors on a trip.

Photograph from the Philippe Garner Collection showing the beach area to the east of the pier, *c.* 1902. Families shelter under their parasols and children paddle. In the foreground a young girl cradles a baby, her hat decorated like an Easter bonnet.

A busy scene on the West Pier, *c.* 1906. Top right can be seen the luxurious Grand Hotel which was built in 1864, a railway boom period. The original cost was £160,000 for nine tiers of rooms with a total of 150 bedrooms. This was the first hotel to have lifts and electric lighting.

On a windy day a paddle-steamer shelters from the inclement weather next to the West Pier, *c.* 1920. A large number of bathing machines are drawn up on the beach.

A postcard home, 1914.

View from the Palace Pier towards the derelict West Pier, which wears an air of faded glory, 1996. It was after the Second World War that the neglect of maintenance started to show its full effect. During 1970 the southern end was closed and in 1975 the pier itself closed. The Brighton West Pier Trust, a registered charity, acquired the ownership of the pier, with the enormous task of saving this fine Victorian Grade I structure. In March 1998 the Heritage Lottery Fund awarded £10 million pounds towards its renovation.

CHAPTER TWO

THE BUILDING OF PALACE PIER

A t noon on 20 May 1899 the Mayoress of Brighton, Mrs Hawkes, performed the opening ceremony of the newly built Brighton Marine Palace and Pier. The *Evening Argus* told its readers that inclement weather and rough seas had failed to deter a considerable crowd of people who had gathered to watch the ceremony. But in spite of the use of a loudspeaker the speech made by Mrs Hawkes was rendered inaudible by the same gale which threatened to destroy the pier's decorative ribbons. That part of the ceremony completed, the Mayoress was followed on to the pier by the Mayor and other members of the Town Council, members of the Pier Company and by prominent townsmen and their families to witness another ceremony at the far end. With the use of a suitably inscribed silver spanner, the Mayoress then declared the first column in place for the pier head upon which the Pavilion was to be completed and opened two years later. In spite of hearing little or nothing of the speeches made by Mrs Hawkes, the crowds upon the pier and the beach replied with three hearty cheers after which a Union Jack was unfurled aloft and the band of the 1st Volunteer Battalion Royal Sussex Regiment played 'God Save the Queen'. The Pier Company then retired to the Music Room of the Royal Pavilion where they entertained their numerous guests to luncheon.

Richard St George Moore had not reached the age of thirty when he was appointed as the architect for the project. He had served a pupillage with Messrs Laird Brothers, Birkenhead, and had since practised on his own account as a civil engineer in Westminster. Moore had been responsible, between 1886 and 1890, for the design and construction of the nearby pier at St Leonards, Sussex, at a cost of £27,000. Although this had been on a smaller scale than the new pier at Brighton was intended to be, its success no doubt clinched his appointment for the larger work.

Moore's pier was to be about 1,000 ft long, 500 ft longer than the West Pier, and with a promenade deck 45 ft wide. The landing stage was sufficiently far from the shore to be used by passenger ships at the lowest tides. The pavilion was to be 170 ft long and, like its counterpart on the West Pier, had an oriental design. It housed a 60 ft long concert hall capable of seating an audience of 1,500 in addition to a dining hall, a private dining-room and a kitchen. Verandas flanked the east and west sides of the construction. Sheltered seating was to be placed at strategic points along the pier and around the pavilion. The whole edifice was to rest upon 330 cast-iron piles above which latticed girders supported the deck.

Construction began in November 1891 by Mayoh Brothers of Manchester, but, as is often the case in large building ventures, the next six years were bedevilled by financial and contractual difficulties. A further act of Parliament was required in 1893 to allow for an extra three years to complete the work under a new construction company, which itself went bankrupt before it had finished a little over 1,000 ft. Yet another act of Parliament was required to extend the construction period and further costs were laid upon the Palace Pier Company when, at the end of 1896, the Chain Pier was washed away and its debris damaged both of the other piers. The future looked bleak for the shareholders of the Palace Pier Company and in the following year the High Court ordered its liquidation. A stay of execution, however, was to be allowed if the company could show that it was capable of discharging its debts. A local benefactor in the person of Sir James Howard stepped forward to save the day and work continued until the opening of the pier in May 1899, with additional parliamentary legislation which allowed a further three years for the completion of the pavilion extension.

The 1890s had witnessed a rapid expansion in the use of electricity to illuminate public places such as theatres, fashionable clubs and restaurants, an expansion that was already replacing the smelly gas-mantles in middle-class homes. It was therefore fitting that, after the daytime ceremonies and celebrations of 20 May 1899, the Palace Pier was illuminated from end to end by over 3,000 light-bulbs. This demonstration of the use of electrical illumination in such an open domain must have had a powerful effect upon all who saw it from the shore and sea. If mankind, especially that of the British variety, could outdo the brilliance of Nature's sunsets, what other wonders would the impending twentieth century have in store for them?

Opposite above: On 7 November 1891 work began on the building of the Palace Pier. The ceremony of driving the first pile was overseen by Alderman S.H. Soper. The cold November day drew a large gathering, but little did they know that the project would be fraught with such financial difficulties and would take over seven years to complete. A military band is positioned behind the top railings to serenade the event. The public could board Magnus Volk's electric railway, the first of its kind opened in 1883, only a few yards away.

CHRONOLOGY OF DEVELOPMENT

1891   7 November. Work started.

1899   20 May. Pier opened to the public.

1899   First piles driven for the pier head.

1901   3 April. Theatre opened.

1906   Windscreen erected centre of deck.

1911   Bandstand opened.

1911   Winter Gardens completed (now the Palace of Fun).

1911   Theatre remodelled with rooftop garden and café added.

1930   Alterations to pier entrance. Canopy and clock tower erected.

1934   Toll houses from Chain Pier re-sited on Palace Pier.

1935   Dodgem Car track built as extension over landing stage.

1937   East Pavilion erected.

1973   Landing stage demolished.

1986   Theatre demolished.

1986   Pier head decking extended.

1986   Palace of Fun renovated.

1986   Dome-shaped structure built at pier head.

R. St. G. Moore, Esq, 1883

Richard St George Moore (1858–1926). This portrait was taken when he was elected as a corporate member of the Institution of Civil Engineers on 4 December 1883. Educated in London and Germany he served his apprenticeship in Birkenhead. In 1885 he carried out the design and construction of Skegness Pier and the sea wall at Bridlington; St Leonard's Pier, 1886–90; Brighton Marine Palace Pier, 1889, the contract for design and construction being costed at £76,000; West Hampshire waterworks, 1892; extension and pavilion for Ryde Pier at a cost of £5,300, 1893. He also designed works for the Brighton and Rottingdean Seashore Electric Tramway, was engineer for the Gigantic Wheel in Paris and worked in Singapore and India. During the First World War, as deputy director in the Special Construction Department of the Admiralty, he designed 800-ft Marconi towers. He was a President of the Society of Engineers.

The new pier at Brighton, designed by Mr R. St George Moore, Assoc. MICE Westminster, Engineer. This drawing appeared in *The Engineer*, 29 January 1892. It was a fantasy interpretation of Moore's plan and not to scale.

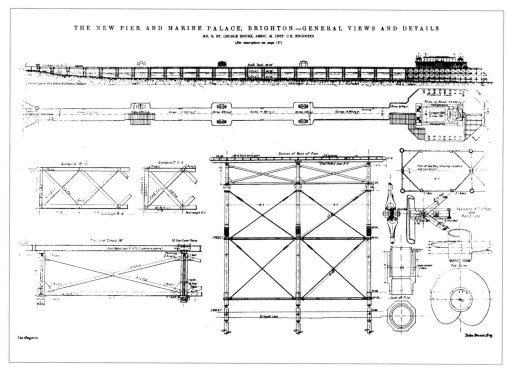

THE NEW PIER AND MARINE PALACE, BRIGHTON.—GENERAL VIEWS AND DETAILS

MR. R. ST. GEORGE MOORE, ASSOC. M. INST. C.E. ENGINEER

Detailed plan, *The Engineer*, 12 February 1892. An estimated 2,000 tons of metal were used in its final construction. The entire structure covered an area of 2½ acres and 85 miles of planking were used.

Work commenced on the Palace Pier in November 1891 and the contract was placed with Mayoh Bros of Manchester, who were experienced pier builders and were involved in a total of seven piers. At one point they had a partnership with the Widnes Foundry Co. This photographic postcard shows work east of the pier head near the landing stage and dates from about 1900. It is interesting to note that in 1899 permission was granted for a train to run the length of the pier with a track gauge of 3 ft 6 in. The venture was not followed through, presumably because of lack of funds.

The unfinished Palace Pier with the Chain Pier in the distance, *c.* 1895. A natural gathering place for children to assemble was under the pier. In later years pennies would be thrown from the pier into the sea for children to retrieve.

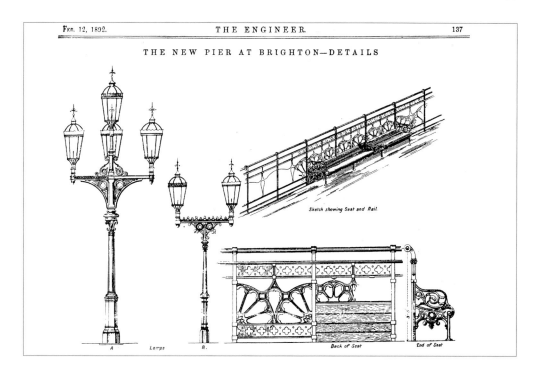

Feb. 12, 1892. THE ENGINEER. 137

THE NEW PIER AT BRIGHTON—DETAILS

Sketch showing Seat and Rail.

A   Lamps   B.   Back of Seat   End of Seat

View of Marine Parade looking west showing the skeleton of the Palace Pier reaching out to sea, with the Chain Pier in the distance, *c.* 1895. Markwell's Hotel is now the Queen's Hotel. Business was obviously slack with the hackney carriages queueing for trade. The picture was taken on a hot afternoon with ladies strolling along the promenade, sheltering under their parasols from the heat of the summer sun.

The men's bathing beach east of the skeleton of the Palace Pier, *c.* 1895. According to *Wards Pictorial & Descriptive Guide to Brighton & Hove*, 'free bathing from the beach is permitted from certain public bathing places, distinguished by notice-boards before eight o'clock in the morning and after eight o'clock in the evening.' Bathing machines were first recorded in use from the 1730s at Scarborough Bay. They were huts on wheels drawn into the sea by a horse. Quaker Benjamin Beale invented the 'Modesty Hood' attachment which was first used at Margate during 1753. Bathers were led from the machines naked with mixed bathing prohibited. The cost of hiring one remained constant at around a shilling for many years. They were in use up to 1914 and could still be seen lingering on our beaches well into the late 1920s.

The Chain Pier on its last legs, *c.* 1896. The Borough Engineer for Brighton had ordered the structure to be closed the previous October after finding the pier head 6 ft 9in out of perpendicular. The Directors of the Chain Pier had reluctantly sold it in 1891 to the Brighton Marine Palace Pier Co. for the sum of £15,000. The shareholders received £13 6s 8d for every £100 share owned and £36 13s 4d in debentures of the new company.

A poster in the window of the Toll-House announces the Royal Chain Pier closure. Veteran shipwright Edward Fogden, who had been employed on the pier for nearly forty years, poses for the camera, his livelihood having been destroyed.

" Beneath the Lowest Deep a Lower Deep."

The following advertisement appeared in a local journal of Friday, December 11th :—

WRECKAGE FROM CHAIN PIER, BRIGHTON, ON THE BEACH, opposite Albion Hotel. TO TIMBER & FIREWOOD DEALERS & OTHERS.
Mr. THOMAS CHAPMAN will Sell by Auction, on MONDAY, December 14th, 1896, at Twelve, 150 LOTS of USEFUL TIMBER, relics of the late-lamented Pier.

The morning after the storm of 4 December 1896. The Board of Trade had already ordered that the Chain Pier be demolished as soon as the Palace Pier was complete. The Chain Pier met its fate, however, at 10.30 p.m. one night well before its neighbour was finished, when it shivered from end to end during a terrific storm. By morning almost nothing remained. The sea was strewn with wreckage and after seventy-three years its existence had come to a sad end. A number of enterprising local artists painted the Chain Pier on wood washed ashore to sell as a reminder of its existence.

Crowds gather the following morning to witness the fate of the Old Chain Pier. The timbers from the wrecked Chain Pier left a trail of havoc causing £2,000 damage to the Palace Pier. The new owners of the Chain Pier had further claims against them from the West Pier for £6,000, it having been cut in half during the storm, and from Volk's Electric Railway for £1,500. The overall result was the near collapse of the Palace Pier project. Only the intervention of Sir John Howard saved the day.

A huge crowd is being entertained on the beach by travelling entertainers 'The Highwaymen', c. 1905. Pierrot and minstrel groups also performed shows; the latter were an import from the USA at the end of the nineteenth century. 'Bottlers' would go round the audience collecting money; this often proved quite a performance in itself!

Repairs to the Pier Head after storm damage,
c. 1913. Pier construction and maintenance were
often frustrated by inclement weather. The work
was hazardous and a sudden storm could destroy
weeks of progress. This photograph shows a
3-ton pile about to be lowered into position.

London builders W.G. Beaumont & Son of the Priory Works, Bow, E3, were contracted to build a new
entrance to the pier in 1930. The photograph shows one side of the pier as the new piles are being sunk. The
tender price was £1,909 8s and the architects were Clayton & Black of Brighton. During the work the 'Lost
River of Brighton' was discovered; it had originally flowed through the Stein. Here the project is being
completed above the tide line, and the clerk of works is talking to Oliver Dalton and another director.

The exuberant, oriental domes on the roof of the Palace Pier Theatre, *c.* 1931. A lone decorator ensures the onion domes will reflect brightly on the Brighton skyline. During the late 1950s the area under the domes was converted into a staff restaurant.

Workmen on the roof of the café, *c.* 1936. The west side of the pier demanded heavier expenditure on maintenance as it took the full force of any stormy westerly weather. Here work is in progress to widen the deck area using 'New Jarrah' hardwood. Messrs Westwards from East London were the structural engineers.

Engineers installing a pulley during deck extension work on the west side of the pier near the theatre, c. 1950.

A team of painters working on the Palace of Fun during the winter of 1950. The 'Toshing' gangs, as they were known, worked below deck in the summer months tarring the piles and above deck in the winter on general painting.

The signal cannon which was fired on the Chain Pier to inform the townsfolk of the arrival of steam packets from France is now situated on the Palace Pier. It was photographed in 1988.

Ornate cast-iron work on the side of the Old Chain Pier toll-house, now sited on the Palace Pier and photographed in July 1993. Now almost 177 years old, it is remarkable that it has survived such a corrosively hostile atmosphere.

CHAPTER THREE

MUSIC

The Palace Pier Theatre was a natural venue for musical concerts and in 1906 Sir Henry Joseph Wood, the founder of the 'Promenade Concerts' at London's Queen's Hall and the composer of operettas and of an oratorio, performed a series of chamber music works. His international reputation had been established by the 'Promenade Concerts' and the pier management and music loving visitors and residents must have felt that his concerts added to the cultural reputation of pier and town alike. There were also some ballet productions. The predominant tone was aimed at family audiences.

When the theatre was enlarged in 1911 the Winter Palace, now known as the Palace of Fun, and the bandstand were also built. These additions improved facilities for giving musical concerts during the week and on Sundays when Sabbatical Laws of the eighteenth century forbade theatrical productions. Again, it was necessary to aim at the tastes of a broad audience and a typical Sunday repertoire of 1913 included works, or excerpts from them, by Verdi, Lehar, Mendelssohn, Mascagni, Brahms, Wagner and the introduction of the composer, hitherto probably unknown to this audience, Jean Sibelius.

The policy of free entry to the pier meant that concerts on the bandstand could be heard by everyone on the pier itself and many people on the promenade, even if a charge was made for the use of the seats around the bandstand itself. Brass bands were the ideal form of music to overcome the noises of the elements, sea-gulls and competing seafront attractions. There was already a long tradition of such bands elsewhere in the British Isles where they were the pastime of colliery, factory and mill workers. In the unindustrialized southern counties, however, the brass bands of the Army and Royal Marines were able to fill the gap when civilian ones were unavailable. Regular appearances were made on the bandstand by the bands of local regiments and the Band of the Grenadier Guards sometimes gave concerts inside the Winter Palace.

The music played on the pier was sometimes 'lightweight' and had to cater for popular tastes with the works of well-established composers. But contemporary composers were introduced and the range of works strongly contradicts Wagner's ill-informed judgement that England was 'a land without music'!

The ceremony of fixing the first column at the Pier Head on 29 May 1899 was performed by the Mayoress of Brighton, Mrs A.J. Hawkes. This ceremony marked the beginning of the construction of the theatre which has since had a long musical tradition. Gale force winds ensured the assembled guests held on to their hats. Photographs such as this provide an interesting vivid insight into social history and are the 'eye of history'.

BRIGHTON PALACE PIER. 162

Under the direction of Mr. Cecil Barth.

Next Sunday, June 2nd, 1901.

GRAND EVENING CONCERT

AT 8 O'CLOCK.

ARTISTES :

Madame Ida Wales.   **Miss Gertrude Macaulay.**
Mr. Henry Beaumont.   **Mr. Ballard Brown.**

| SOLO VIOLIN | .. | .. | .. | .. | MISS DOROTHEA WALENN. |
| ACCOMPANIST | .. | .. | .. | .. | MR. ARTHUR W. BRIGGS. |

Madame IDA WALES.
(Soprano Vocalist.)

DOORS OPEN AT 7.30.

PRICES:—Reserved Stalls, 2s.; Stalls, 1s.; Admission 6d. Private
Boxes 10s. 6d. and 15s.

Seats can be booked at Messrs. LYON and HALLS, Messrs. R. POTTS and
Co's, and at the Pier.

A LIMITED NUMBER OF FREE ADMISSIONS TO THE PAVILION.

Theatre poster, 2 June 1901. The Palace Pier Theatre opened on Wednesday 3 April 1901. The Sacred Harmonic Society were the first performers, with George Foreman conducting the Pavilion Orchestra. There was an invited audience of 1,500 guests and tea was served afterwards. The seating was tiered while the stage was capacious, with Moorish-style arches. The building housed shops, refreshment rooms and reading rooms. During 1911 the theatre was remodelled, a circle and boxes were added and the stage enlarged, with a new seating capacity of 1,300. Initially lantern slides were popular, but as the cinema developed they retired into graceful obscurity.

Posted on 3 October 1903, this splendid postcard shows Karl Kaps' Famous Light Cavalry Military Band. They are posing outside the theatre – one can imagine their musical repertoire. The advertisement at the top of the page is from around the same year.

Palace Pier at night, 1906. Mr M. Fileman, an electrical engineer operating from 99 Queens Road, Brighton, installed 3,500 lights. In 1906 Henry J. Wood (1869–1944) founder of the London Proms, toured a number of smaller halls with his quintet. An advertisement at the pier entrance shows he was conducting at 3.30 p.m. and 8.30 p.m. on a Sunday. Professor A. Jacobs, in his book *The Making of the Proms*, describes Wood as 'contributing with distinction to British musical life, the secret of his success lying in his tireless creativity and his gigantic enthusiasm.'

An advertisement at the pier entrance shows the Northumberland Hussars were to play at the bandstand, *c.* 1911. Business was brisk. Ronald Dalton recalls how when the military bands performed 'a bugler was dispatched to the entrance to advertise the concert'. Ronald, born in 1916, is the only surviving son of Oliver Dalton (*see* p. 92). Educated at Cranley Public School, he eventually became the pier's Assistant Manager.

The newly erected bandstand, *c.* 1911. Mr H.G. Amers, the Bandmaster, is seen on the right conducting the String Band of the Northumberland Hussars at a morning performance, which commenced at 11.30 with a 'Surprise Programme' including a 'Humorous Selection . . . Melodious Morceaux and Intermezzos and Solos for Cello, Violin, Cornet and Vocal Recitals'. The bandstand had an enclosure which, in theory, sheltered the patrons from all winds and weather. The elegantly dressed ladies in the foreground are dedicated followers of fashion with flowers decorating their hats.

The five-man Palace Pier Jazz Band posing against a background of tropical plants in the Winter Gardens, *c.* 1913.

Popular Bandmaster Mr H. G. Amers strolls the deck. Promoted to Captain in 1917 he returned from the First World War a wounded hero and was invited to take the baton for one last concert. During 1929 the cost of hiring the Scots Guards Band was £300 a week. In order to cut back on the expense of having to hire large bands the 'Lafleur' organ was introduced in 1939, the first organist being Colin Mann.

The Municipal Orchestra of twenty-six performers played at the Aquarium during the winter. In the summer as well as playing on the Palace Pier they performed at the Stein Gardens, the Pavilion Grounds and at Preston Park. They are seen here in about 1928.

Entertaining in the Palace Pier Bandstand, Teddy Hayes conducts his swing band on 21 April 1934. They made daily appearances during that season. Other famous bands who appeared on the Pier included the Southern Syncopated, Debroy Somers and Jack Hylton, who were always greeted with 'House Full' boards.

CHAPTER FOUR

THE PALACE PIER THEATRE

The extension was completed ahead of time and in April 1901 the ornate Palace Pier Theatre was opened. It was enlarged ten years later to give it a seating capacity of 1,300 and was the venue for musicals, comedy drama, variety shows and pantomimes until its destruction in 1973.

Before the outbreak of war in 1914, along with the ever popular operettas of Gilbert and Sullivan, Edward German's *Merrie England* was also produced. Other musical comedies included Paul Rubens's *The Balkan Princess* and Leslie Stuart's exotic *Floradora*. The well-known dramatic farce by Arthur Pinero, *Dandy Dick*, was brought from the West End in 1901 and the tendency to show established works was still evident in 1913 with Jerome K. Jerome's *Robina in Search of a Husband*. Both dramatists were familiar to the public and, as winter winds blew along the English Channel, audiences were persuaded to take the third of a mile walk along the pier to see the plays. Perched above the waves and making adjustments to suit the three-month summer holiday season, the Palace Pier Theatre took on the role of a typical provincial playhouse. It depended largely upon touring companies that brought with them successful works from the capital.

Music-hall variety shows were a feature of the summer season with visiting performers as well as resident troupes such as the 'Palace Pier Follies'. Music halls were an essential part of Victorian and Edwardian public entertainment and survived until after the Second World War, when the combined forces of the cinema, radio and television replaced them. Before the 1930s few could have foreseen the changes that electrical power would eventually bring in the form of mass entertainment. The impresario Jack Sheppard's concert party 'The Entertainers' and Jimmy Hunter's 'Brighton Follies' were typical of their day. Some of the earliest appearances of Max Miller were made on the Palace Pier with these troupes. But the training of these entertainers was for this medium alone and when concert parties eventually ceased to exist few had the opportunity to transfer elsewhere.

After 1911 occasional use of the theatre was made for the showing of early feature and short drama films, although it was never used exclusively as a cinema. Its multi-purpose nature is also well demonstrated when we see that on at least one occasion it housed a circus performance, although how easily the animals were conveyed along the length of the pier is not recorded.

The reopening of the theatre after the Second World War seemed to herald its renaissance but, with the general trend of provincial theatres, it declined as the years passed. Visiting repertory companies continued and the impresario Myles Byrne presented the young Dick Emery, Tommy Trinder and Ronnie Corbett to his audiences. A nostalgic revival of music-hall brought some relief and enabled holidaymakers to see the radio stars Elsie and Doris Walters. Theirs was the last performance in the theatre before it was severely damaged by the collision of a barge in 1973.

Opposite top: Interior of the Palace Pier Theatre viewed towards the stage, *c.* 1911. *Bottom*: Interior of the Palace Pier Theatre viewed from the stage, *c.* 1911. The decor at the time was royal blue, cream and gold. The theatre had a ventilation system that could cool the atmosphere in the summer by pumping in cold sea air. The interior was described as a 'revelation' and the acoustics were near perfect.

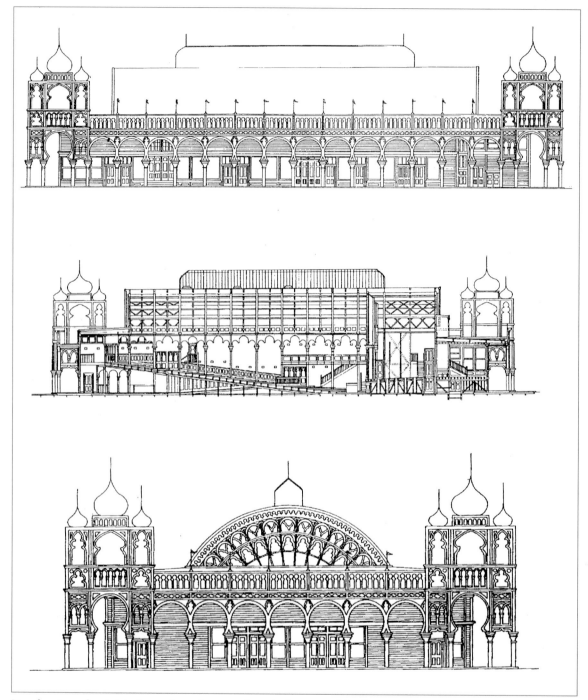

Line drawings of east, interior sections of west, and north elevations of the theatre.

Fashionable strollers promenade outside the front entrance of the theatre, *c.* 1911. Note the popularity of straw boaters for men and ankle-length skirts for the ladies. The poster (top) advertising Easter Monday's attractions is from pre-1920.

From 1910 onward the theatre had a rival which was soon to grow into a serious financial competitor – the cinematograph, bioscope or animatograph. This was especially popular in Brighton because the Hove film pioneers, Smith and Williamson, had introduced their moving pictures locally as early as 1901. Local historian John Montgomery wrote in his article 'Our Pier Theatres' (1978) that 'travelling showmen gave short programmes of moving pictures, particularly "topicals" or actuality films, which became popular after the scenes from the Boer War were screened.' Silent films were succeeded by talkies after 1929.

Photographic postcard, *c.* 1911. *Floradora* was being performed at the theatre with the band of HM 2nd Dragoon Guards on the bandstand. The sea-front was busy with vendors doing a brisk trade. The level of horse-drawn transport was still significant at this time.

The Palace Pier Follies were a hard-working group. In 1917 they performed three times a day and twice on Sundays. Below is a bill for a play typical of the shows staged at the theatre.

PALACE PIER BRIGHTON.

General Manager   -   -   J. W. CORDINER

MONDAY, AUGUST 1st, 1921,

EVERY EVENING AT 8.

MONDAY, WEDNESDAY and SATURDAY at 3.

MACDONALD & YOUNG

PRESENT

PEG O' MY HEART

A COMEDY OF YOUTH IN THREE ACTS

By J. HARTLEY MANNERS.

Characters in Order of their Appearance.

Mrs. Chichester	... ENA DOUGLAS
Jarvis, ...	W. G. BLUNT
Ethel, Mrs. Chichester's Daughter	KATHLEEN CHRISTOPHER
Alaric, Mrs. Chichester's Son ...	... H. E. GARDEN
Christian Brent	..., CYRIL VERNON
" Peg "	... IDA ROSALIE
Montgomery Hawkes, Solicitor ...	WILLIAM YELDHAM
Bennett — — ...	MARIE DAVENTRY
Jerry ... — ...	RICHARD CUSTANCE

Scene—A Room in Regal Villa, Mrs. Chichester's House,
Scarborough

Act 1	-	-	-	The Coming of Peg
Act 2	-	-	-	The Rebellion of Peg
Act 3	-	-	-	Peg o' My Heart

Mermaid Theatre programme, 1922. *A Little Bit of Fluff* was being performed at the theatre in July of that year. During 1929 the heating and ventilation system in the theatre was upgraded at a cost of £300.

Pantomime programme, c. 1930. The entertainment was characterised by music, lavish sets, stock role and topical jokes. Most pantomimes lasted for four or five weeks. Many local children and families went to several shows in the town paying between 6d and 2s. The pantomimes were always good money spinners. The Palace Pier produced one every year for twenty-one consecutive years up to the Second World War.

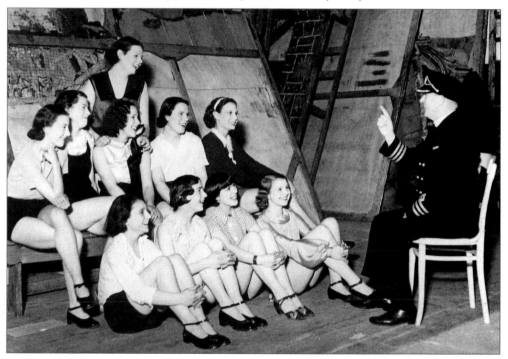

This behind-the-scenes photograph shows Piermaster Weeks sharing a funny story with the pantomime girls during Christmas 1934.

Front cover of a theatre programme, 17 June 1938.

Tuesday, DECEMBER 26th, 1939, and onwards

TWICE DAILY AT 2 AND 7 P.M.

HARRY BENET

presents his Delightful Pantomime

"DICK WHITTINGTON"

AND HIS CAT

Book by H. Flockton Foster.   Original Music by Cyril Dawson.

Ballets and Ensembles by Ann Renova.   Costumes by Kandy, London.

THE PANTOMIME PRODUCED BY FREDDY PAYNE

under the personal direction of HARRY BENET

CAST :

Dick Whittington ...	RENEE REEL
Alice Fitzwarren ...	PEGGY PAYNE
Idle Jack ...	FREDDY PAYNE
Alderman Fitzwarren	FRED KITCHEN, Jr
Selina, The Cook	JOE LIPTON
Tommy, The Cat	CHRIS RAPIER
Captain and Mate	ALLEN & TAYLOR
Emperor of Morocco	HARRY FREARSON
King Rat	ALEC HARDY
Fairy Starlight	MARY LOWE
Cuthbert	CLIVE GAY

Specialities by :

DODO BANKS ELSTREE BABES   **THE IDA LILLE GIRLS**

LES RAPIERS   **ANN RENOVA**

ALLEN & TAYLOR   **FOUR CARLTON SINGERS**

THE

4 BOBRICS 4

(The Act Unique)

CHRIS AMBROSE AND HIS BAND

Scene 1	THE BELFRY
Scene 2	OLD CHEAPSIDE
Scene 3	HEADING FOR FITZWARREN'S STORES
Scene 4	INTERIOR OF THE STORES
Scene 5	ON THE WAY TO HIGHGATE
Scene 6	HIGHGATE HILL
Scene 7	THE FAIRY GLEN

INTERVAL

Scene 8	THE PORT OF LONDON
Scene 9	BETWEEN DECKS
Scene 10	DECK OF THE SHIP
Scene 11	THE SHORES OF MOROCCO
Scene 12	THE COURTYARD OF THE EMPEROR'S PALACE
Scene 13	A STREET IN OLD LONDON
Scene 14	THE GUILDHALL

Pantomime *Dick Whittington*, 26 December 1939. It looks as though the show must go on: war had been declared on 3 September 1939. The theatre was not closed until 23 May 1940.

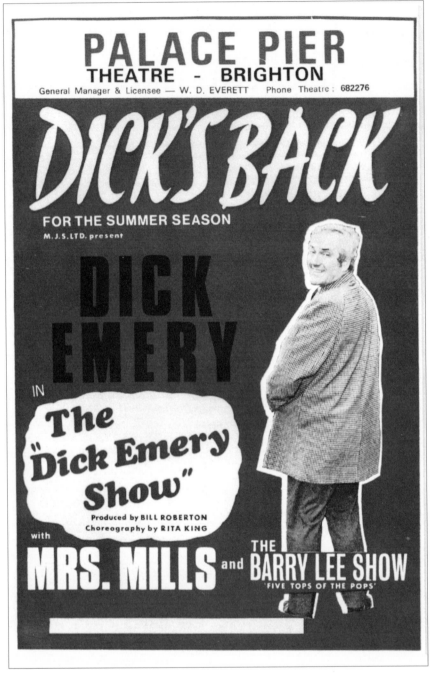

Programme from the Dick Emery summer season on the pier, 1970. The show had returned from the previous year because of popular demand. Comedian Dick Emery came from a show-business family and his link-up with Michael Bentine in *It's a Square World* gave him his major breakthrough. The BBC television series *The Dick Emery Show* in 1964 was a smash hit and gave him international recognition. Other artists on the show included Mrs Mills, who played the piano and was first seen on the *Billy Cotton Band Show*. The *Barry Lee Show* was performed by a musical comedy band, similar to the Barron Knights. A young ventriloquist, Keith Harris, is mentioned inside the programme; he later found fame with his puppet Orville.

'Music Hall at the Palace Pier', 1973 season. This was the last show to be performed in the theatre prior to damage sustained when a barge collided with it. Top of the bill were Elsie and Doris Waters, better known as 'Gert and Daisy'; they had found fame in early BBC radio shows. Sandy Powell enjoyed record sales of over 7 million copies. His famous catchphrase was 'Can you hear me Mother?' Brighton had a long tradition of music-hall performances but alas they are no more.

Permission was given in 1973 to demolish the landing stage which had been used by fishermen but had become unsafe and uneconomical to repair. No paddle-steamers had come alongside for a number of years. During the removal of the landing stage a sudden storm blew up on Friday 19 October 1973. An 80-ft, 50-ton Thames lighter barge that had been moored to the landing stage broke free from its mooring ropes.

A total of twenty-five piles were smashed by the barge, causing ironwork, docking and buildings above, including the helter-skelter, to collapse. The north-west corner of the theatre sagged approximately 2 ft. It was described by W.D. Everett, the General Manager, as a 'tricky engineering feat to jack the building back into place'. The cost of the damage was estimated at £1 million, for which there was no insurance cover.

The Palace Pier Theatre started to break up, but the toilet on the right was miraculously saved.

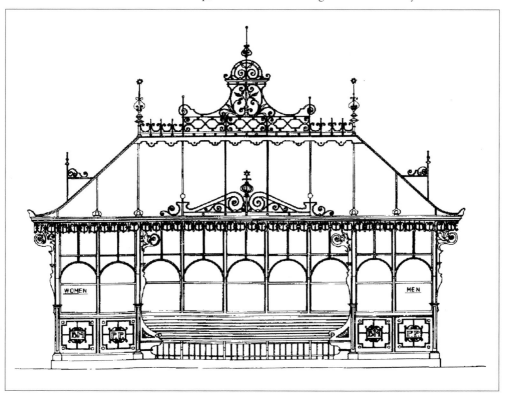

A line drawing of the toilet showing the fine detailed ironwork, which still survives today.

Aerial view, November 1973. The full extent of the total damage can now be seen as the pier head reaches out on a calm sea.

In 1986, thirteen years after the accident, the theatre was demolished. When the safety curtain came down for the last time, only the haunting memory of yesteryear remained, the audience's laughter and tears echoing in the rubble.

CHAPTER FIVE

AMUSEMENTS

ll piers attract devotees of the sport of angling and it was constantly practised on the Palace Pier free of charge until it was banned in 1984. The Brighton Palace Pier and District Anglers Association entertained other clubs to competitions from an early date at all times of the year, regardless of the weather. Newspaper reports from the 1930s record the sighting of small sharks in the sea at Brighton but whether anybody caught one is not mentioned. It is certain that few anglers could have been more surprised at their catch than the holidaymaker who landed a lady's handbag on to the Palace Pier during the summer of 1938. Captain F.C. Weeks, the Piermaster then and for nearly thirty years after, succeeded in tracing its owner to her home in Brixton. She had lost it in the sea more than a month before!

By the late nineteenth century fashions in entertainment were changing along with the ability of industry to produce coin-operated vending and peep-show machines. The mechanical or clockwork action could be triggered by dropping a coin into machines which were becoming more complex and were able to perform other tasks than simply turning the drum of a pianola. Many of the ideas had come from the United States and some machines that were manufactured by the International Mutoscope Reel Company, USA, just after the First World War were still in use fifty years later. The Palace Pier was a natural recipient of these coin-operated machines which were to become almost an obligatory part of an excursion from London. One penny could reveal the secrets of 'What the Butler Saw', 'The Execution of Mary Queen of Scots' or 'The Haunted House'. Some of the scenes were rapidly moving photographs which, on the same principle of the illusion of 'moving pictures', presented a short drama that was capable of shocking only in what it suggested rather than in what was actually revealed. Some were displays of animated models which depicted, for instance, the scene of a scaffold upon which the figures moved towards the block and were decapitated at the appropriate moment. (Sex and violence are not exclusively modern preoccupations.) Other machines told fortunes on a pre-printed card for those who were gullible enough to believe them. Others still, working on a belief widely held since the early nineteenth century that electric shocks could cure a variety of illnesses, subjected those who were not too timid to a current of low voltage through the hands. (At least one hopes it was a low voltage!)

These early examples of automation, next to the helter-skelter and the ferris wheel, replaced some human labour in that individual performers such as musicians, jugglers and fire-eaters had less room to perform along the pier once the machines had been installed. The machines were more profitable because payment was obligatory. Other machines dispensed cigarettes, matches and chocolate, as they did on railway stations, but they could not cope with a lot of the traditional seaside fare such as ice-cream, toffee-apples and rock. Still less could they easily be adapted to sell postcards, through which visitors browsed as if in a public lending library, or the ever popular chinaware that provided mementoes of the visit. This was either too fragile or bulky to be sold other than by kiosk assistants who, like many other workers on the pier and elsewhere in the resort, were employed just for the season. Nevertheless, the inroad that machines had begun to make upon employment, although minute by later standards, was the beginning of a process that has become a major social problem in our own times.

The portable box camera was well established by the Edwardian period, but for many it was an important part of the holiday ritual to be 'snapped' on the promenade or the pier by those who were regarded as 'professionals'. This was a souvenir that not only supplied first-hand evidence of the visit, but enabled the subjects to show off what they were wearing and who they were with. The varied amusements of the pier provided its visitors with a release from the boredom of routine in the office, behind the shop counter, the factory bench or the warehouse at a time when normal working hours were far in excess of what they are today and annual paid holidays but a fraction. It was a release too from the drudgery of still unmechanized household work at home, or 'in service', which made virtual slaves of all but the privileged few of the nation's women well into the twentieth century.

Bathing beauty competitions, including the event to select Miss Brighton, and other contests such as the Ladies' Ankle Competition, were a feature of the pier during those years between the death of Victorian prudery and the advent of a more sinister prudery in the form of 'political correctness'. Such events were an important part of the Brighton Carnival during the summer season and entertained visitors and competitors alike, all of whom were ignorant of the 'degrading spectacle' that this sort of behaviour represented.

Visitors also had access to a growing number of coin-slot operated machines along the pier, many of which had been produced in the United States, of fun-fair rides, shooting galleries, ice-cream and confectionery stalls, and opportunities to take either alcoholic or non-alcoholic refreshments. The 1920s and 1930s witnessed the Palace Pier's maximum commercial development and number of visitors, a period now recognized as its 'golden years'.

In addition to the fun-fair, other facilities catered for casual visitors such as day-trippers, whose early departure prevented them from attending the evening concert or play. A precedent had been set by the owners of the Old Chain Pier, who had learnt the commercial value of casual entertainment by letting kiosks to sellers of souvenirs and refreshments, and to fortune-tellers.

Whatever the conditions of employment or domesticity, the amusements also provided an escape from the constraints of adulthood and enabled men and women, albeit for an hour or two, to laugh and behave as they had in childhood. Perhaps the pier's off-shore location encouraged visitors to see it as a 'Never-Never Land' which was inhabited, not by the Red Indians and pirates of *Peter Pan*, but by the amusements of the slot-machines and kiosks. For a brief while adult cares and responsibilities could be safely abandoned within sight of the 'real world' of England.

A group of Brighton fishermen pose among the trappings of their declining business, *c.* 1895. In the distance behind the forest of masts and sails the unfinished Palace Pier can be seen. Space on the beach between the two piers was already at a premium as boats and bathing machines jostled for position.

The promenade at the entrance to the Palace Pier became a magnet for a number of seaside trades as shown in the foreground of this photograph, *c.* 1900. The Hokey Pokey sellers (ice-cream) began almost as a monopoly of Italian immigrants clustered in the Saffron Hill area of London. 'Their gaily painted carts were to be seen wherever a crowd was expected.' (Anthony Hern, *The Seaside Holiday*, 1967) Also in evidence were hot chestnut sellers, goat chaises (carrying up to four children) for 1*s* an hour, and hackney cabs. The Palace Pier Theatre was almost complete by this time but the wagon roof with its single-arched sweep was yet to be finished.

A Sunday stroll, *c.* 1901. This photographic postcard looking down the deck from the theatre shows the fine filigree archways. The pier was sparsely developed with only a few amusement machines sited next to the outer railings. On the extreme right is a Mechanical Trading Co. 'Gripper' machine. The pier was still very much a place to be seen promenading. The age of more commercial activity, however, was just around the corner.

Bertha & Sames

I should think about the most unique card in your collection. Those faces Brighton pier has to put up with every morning – The visitors list is decidedly shorter this week than last.

Honeymoon couple – they look so happy. This delightful photographic postcard, dated 10 October 1902, was taken on the Palace Pier during the honeymoon of Herbert and Bertha Sames. The card was produced using the American Art Rapid Photography technique. The couple had married on 1 October and the card was sent to Bertha's sister living at the family home in Upper Clapton Road, London. Herbert was an architect and the marriage produced two children, Guy and Vivien. The family moved from London to Westcliff, Essex, and during the late 1930s they settled in Brighton at Cavendish Street, near the West Pier. We wonder how many romantic liaisons on the pier have occurred before and after marriage?

This postcard, printed in Berlin, was posted on 19 September 1904. At that time the pier toll was 3*d*. The lighting provided a dazzling effect described by those who saw it as 'almost dreamlike and magical'. The first directors of the completed Palace Pier were Frank and William Irvine, George Wallis, Richard Baker and John Howard. The capital invested was £150,000 in 15,000 £10 shares, with authorization to borrow a further £50,000.

This George Ruff photograph was taken during 1904 from the west looking past the jetty towards the pier. The children gathered on the lower esplanade as the crowd threw coins for them to scramble over. At the front of the group are barefoot, ill-clad children. Behind the prosperity of the sea-front existed dwellings with appalling conditions. Brighton had its share of working-class slums with poor drainage, narrow streets and overcrowding.

The beach area to the east of the pier, *c.* 1904. An overdressed Edwardian family have an audience, including a dog, as father adjusts his daughter's hair with mother looking sternly on.

Postcard dated 3 June 1904. The enduring appeal of the early years was the 'fresh air and music'. The Palace Pier was probably seen as better value for money as it was longer than the West Pier. Eventually a social divide existed between the two piers. The West became popular with the middle classes and the Palace was used by the day-tripping working classes. On the extreme left of the postcard is a fortune-teller amusement machine with a chocolate vending machine on the right.

Brighton beach, 1905, (crayon, watercolour and gouache on grey paper 30.2 × 29.9 cm). English artist Horace Mann Livens (1862–1936) painted this scene of the beach east of the Palace Pier looking past the bathing machines towards the aquarium and the Royal Albion Hotel. He also studied in Paris and Antwerp where at one point he shared lodgings with Vincent Van Gogh. He was particularly influenced by Claude Monet.

A tranquil Edwardian scene as customers relax in the sunshine on the west side of the theatre, c. 1905. A collection of amusement machines including cast-iron Mutoscopes and a rare Mathewson 'Cricketer' tempt the patrons. In the foreground a mother reads a newspaper as her baby sits upright watching the world go by.

The Styles family ran the 'Cave Café' under the Palace Pier, *c.* 1905. A good pot of tea could be purchased for 6*d.* Business must have been good as the Styles eventually expanded their enterprise, running a fruit and vegetable stall and bowling alley on the pier itself. The family still live in the Brighton area and continue as wholesale fruit and vegetable merchants.

Crowds gather on the groyne to the east of the pier to watch as huge waves crash around, *c.* 1905. Rough seas have always proved a popular fascination with visitors. The power of the sea was never to be underestimated. The weather played a decisive part in the pier's financial success: a sudden shower would drive the holidaymakers off the beaches and on to the pier.

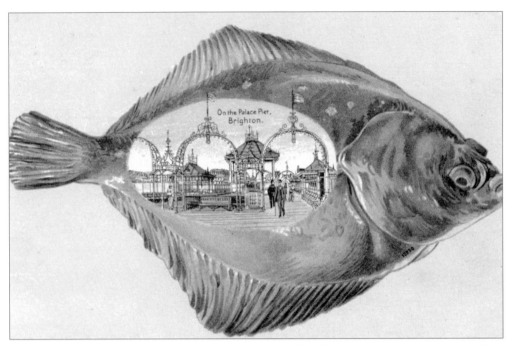

This plaice novelty postcard was posted on 12 September 1905. The series was produced as part of the Boots Cash Chemist Pelham Series.

Hearty Greetings from Brighton, a typical seaside postcard, c. 1906. This type of card captured much of the established folklore of the English seaside holiday.

A proud pose from the Palace Pier nightwatchman, *c.* 1906. He would cycle the deck on his rounds. There was a great fear of fire because so much wood was used in the construction of the pier and he needed to be vigilant. The photograph was taken on the west side of the theatre. An impressive display of amusement machines behind await modest penny coins. Machines right to left are 'The Maze' manufactured by Hayden Bros of Grays Inn Road, London, 'Card Giving Fortune-Teller' possibly by Argyle Auto Co. of London, 'Chocolate Vending' machine and a 'Skill Wall Machine'. Commercial amusement machines were to some degree a symbol of a new cultural order.

Celebrated animated machine-maker, Nelson Abysinnia Lee, *c.* 1898. He was born in Gloucester in 1869 and lived and worked in Blackpool until his death in 1943 at the age of seventy-four years. He was assisted in his business by his wife and son, Leonard. Specializing in animated models, he was influenced by model-maker Dennison. His machines were exhibited at various trade exhibitions in the north of England from 1895 to 1918. He retired at the age of fifty-eight and decided to sell the contents of his amusement arcade at 133 South Promenade, Blackpool. Among the machines were seventeen mechanical models which Oliver Dalton purchased in 1927 for £600. They proved to be a great attraction on the Palace Pier until they were sold in 1971 to a private collector. We have been unable to trace any relatives of Nelson Lee.

The Lady Palmist by Nelson Lee. Using the brass pointer a customer could ask a question, for example 'How will our courtship end?', then pop a penny in the slot. The answer would appear in the fire-place – 'Rest content, happiness is at hand' – followed by a printed card (bottom left) with further predictions. Nelson Lee had a fine eye for detail and the ideas for the various machines were his own. The machines' ultimate popularity with the public was judged at the time by the daily takings. The machines were fitted with handles so they could be carried and used in travelling shows.

The animated machines were driven by powerful spring clockwork motors which were purchased in England. In 1967 A.V. Sheppard, author of a number of pamphlets, described the workings of these machines in detail: 'from this mechanism trains, cranks, spur wheels, levers and cords transmit various motions to the model. The performance is usually over in little less than a minute.' They would need to be wound more than four times a day during the summer season.

Close-up detail from The Lady Palmist. The doll's head is made of bisque china. Mr Peter Grilli of Dover has a collection of four of the original animated machines. One remains unaccounted for from the first batch of machines purchased by Oliver Dalton in 1927 and sold in 1971 – the 'Haunted Churchyard'.

'The Mysterious House. Such mysterious things happened that Perkins did not eat his supper after all.' A rakish man is sitting at a meal in a Jacobean hall. The table utensils and Chinese ornaments are dolls' house equipment and under-scaled for his 12-in figure. The long-case clock strikes and opens revealing a devil, and the cupboard holds a ghost. Two pictures, Victorian photo-portraits, tilt; there is also an oleograph of Warwick Castle. The portrait bust of Beethoven swivels. Meanwhile Perkins' head turns to look at these phenomena.

The Original Anglo-American Bicycle Polo Team, Palace Pier, 1907. Bicycle sports were very popular and this act performed their routine, including the 'Great Bicycle Dive', up to five times a day.

Edwardian Brighton. Entrepreneur Harry Preston came to Brighton from Bournemouth in 1901 to take over the Royal York Hotel. This advertising card, dated 1910, shows the illuminated Palace Pier. In 1913 he took control of the Royal Albion Hotel which had been empty for many years. Brighton being very dear to his heart, he helped promote a plan to resurface the Madeira Drive which enabled motor speed trials to take place.

The bandstand with windscreens and the entrance to the bathing rooms, *c*. 1911. For those bathers who preferred a dip in the open sea, dressing rooms with hot and cold showers were provided. They opened daily from 6 a.m. to 6 p.m. A Dr Whittle wrote at the time: 'facing the east, the dressing rooms are warmed by the morning sun, the open windows disclose the lovely picture of a fleet of trawlers and Brighton cobbles at rest. Cheerful and bright surroundings enhance the pleasure of a dip.' The area also had a gymnasium for which a season ticket cost one guinea and a single ticket 6*d*.

Timetable of entertainments for Tuesday 5 September 1911. The action-packed programme cost 1*d*. On that day two paddle-steamers – the *Brighton Queen* and the *Glen Rosa* – plied for custom. The exploits of 'Dare-Devil Dorothy' and her colleagues would have been interesting to witness. The programme describes the Palace Pier as the most 'modern and magnificent in the world'.

SEPT. 5.	**TUESDAY.**	1911.
A.M.		
9. 0 ...	Pier opens to general public.	
10.10 ...	"Brighton Queen" leaves for Eastbourne, Hastings and Folkestone.	
11.30 ...	Morning Performance of the String Band of the Northumberland Hussars. Vocalist—MR. W. TOPLISS GREEN.	
11.45 ...	Morning Performance of **Palace Pier Entertainers** at head of Pier.	
P.M.		
12.15 ...	Iced drinks of all descriptions can be obtained at the buffet.	
1. 0 ...	Special Luncheons in Restaurant from 1/6.	
2. 0 ...	Fine view of Channel obtained from Pier Head. Comfortable deck chairs.	
3. 0 ...	"Glen Rosa" leaves for Eastbourne.	
3.15 ...	Afternoon Performance of the Military Band of the Northumberland Hussars.	
3.30 ...	Afternoon Performance of **Palace Pier Entertainers** at head of Pier.	
4.30 ...	Teas served on Roof Gardens. Lifts from Deck	
7. 0 ...	Dinner at Restaurant. Table d'Hote from 3/6. Roof Gardens for Refreshment and Wines.	
8. 0 ...	Evening Performance of the Military Band of the Northumberland Hussars.	
8. 0 ...	Performance in Theatre of "**Dare-Devil Dorothy.**" Specialities by Miss Dorothy Richardson, Miss Cissie Williams, "The Two Niros," Miss May Warden, Mr. Deane Cliffe, and Mr. Percy Cahill.	
8.15 ...	Evening Performance of **Palace Pier Entertainers** at head of Pier.	
11. 0 ...	Pier closes.	

Smartly dressed Edwardian ladies and gentlemen enjoying tea on the Roof Garden, *c.* 1911. We hope that the ladder positioned on the extreme left was not for emergency use.

The splendid Roof Tea Garden was built in 1911 when the theatre was remodelled. Two lifts from the deck carried customers up and the teas cost 6*d* for each person. This photographic postcard is dated 15 September 1913.

The Palace Pier Restaurant situated above the theatre entrance, *c.* 1911. The 'luxuriously appointed' restaurant served luncheons from 1*s* 6*d* and dinners (Table d'Hôte) at 2*s* 6*d* and 3*s* 6*d*. A fine selection of old wines and Havana cigars complemented the meals.

Families paddle east of the Palace Pier at low tide, *c.* 1911. A large crowd is gathered on the pier to watch the spectacle.

'Fine Morning For a Row', Raphael Tuck & Sons oilette postcard, *c.* 1911. The heyday for sending postcards in England was from 1900 to 1918 but especially after 1902 when it became legal for messages as well as addresses to be written on the backs of cards, allowing pictures to cover their front. A collecting mania swept the country. Many competent artists were employed to paint coastal scenes for reproduction.

The Palace Pier Entertainers performed at the pier head at 11.45 a.m., 3.30 p.m. and 8.15 p.m., *c.* 1911. This type of pierrot concert party also frequented the beach between the two piers. Here they benefit from the sophisticated surroundings of the Palace Pier with a seated audience.

Interior of the Winter Gardens, *c.* 1912. The architect for the project, completed in 1911, was Mr C.E. Clayton of Brighton. The Winter Gardens were a seaside version of the Crystal Palace and were used for dances and concerts. The first bands to play included The Fascinators and the New Vaudeville Co. The building could be described as a warm barn-like structure filled with palm trees and banks of flowers. It provided a welcome retreat for socialising. It could be quickly transformed into a tea room, with a string trio in the background swooping through a selection of popular music and was a genteel retreat from the harshness of the English weather. During the early 1920s games were organized, such as 'Swanee River' which included a waterfall with a flight of swans which customers caught with rod and line for prizes. During the 1930s a yo-yo contest was organized on the dance floor twice daily.

This biplane was produced by Henry & Maurice Farman and is seen here on a postcard posted on 7 August 1913. It had a 70 hp Renault engine. From 1914 aviation devoted itself almost entirely to war. These biplanes were intended as gun buses. Their pilots were brave men. From 1914 to 1919 the army nominally controlled the pier structure and numerous precautionary measures were taken. A lookout was posted at the pier head, and sentries patrolled the deck at night. Sandbags were placed along the rails and mines were wired in readiness to demolish sections of the pier in the event of invasion.

The Palace Pier advertised on a Brighton & Hove bus, 29 May 1913. Up to forty passengers could have been conveyed to its destination – Sackville Road, Hove.

This silver service menu dated 1914 conjures up a wonderful feast designed to delight the eye and satisfy lovers of French cuisine. How commercially successful it was is hard to tell. This kind of service finished at the Palace Pier Restaurant in 1928. Tradition gave way to market forces and to the day-trippers' meat and two veg! The dinner advertised here could be had for 4*s*, against an average unskilled man's weekly wage of £1 rising to 30*s* for the skilled. A certain ambience must have been created with the Imperial Ladies' Orchestra serenading diners.

Postcard dated 3 August 1917. Bathing machines declined in number during the First World War this was partly because a large number of horses that pulled them in peacetime were used for military purposes.

'Professor' Jack Hurst performs a 60 ft hand balance dive from the Palace Pier, c. 1919. Obviously popular, he came back for the 1920 and 1921 seasons. For some obscure reason aquatic dare-devils often prefixed their names with the title 'Professor'.

Brighton Carnival, 1922.

Huge crowds came to see Brighton's annual carnivals. The Palace Pier staged various entertainments to celebrate this event. Brighton was influenced by foreign competition, and sought to emulate the French Riviera where carnivals were popular. The first Brighton carnival took place in 1922 over a four-day period. It included a 'Battle of Flowers', a decorated procession of commercial vehicles and a firework display. The above postcard dated 19 June 1923 was sent by Aunty Amy. The message reads: 'Did you see anything in London to equal this. This tram was all dark green ferns and pink roses. In the evening it was lit up by hundreds of electric lights all colours. Do you wonder I'm not ready to come home yet.'

The staff of Southern Amusements preparing for an outing, 1930. Because of the restricted Sunday trading laws, Oliver Dalton, pictured centre with bow tie, would treat his staff to outings at the end of the week. The pier was split into two trading companies for tax purposes: Southern Amusements Trading Co., incorporated on 26 January 1923, and the Brighton Marine Palace Pier Co., trading up to 1948. Sir William Gentle became Oliver Dalton's partner in Southern Amusements Trading Co. during 1923.

The entire management and staff of the Palace Pier, May 1931. Pictured at the centre of the bottom row is the Managing Director, Oliver Dalton. Over 160 members of staff are in this photograph.

Piermaster Weeks with members of the Baby Beams child dance troupe who were performing in pantomime on 30 December 1931. The photograph is signed from Joey and Billy to Captain Weeks. During that year a Graf Zeppelin airship flew over the pier on 18 August. These hydrogen-filled airships with a ridged keel were first built by Count Von Zeppelin (1838–1912) during 1900. They were used in the First World War to bomb England. Following a series of disasters in the 1920s and 1930s they were abandoned.

Photographic novelty postcard, c. 1932. This type of card captured the boozy naughtiness identified with having a smashing holiday. Many working-class trippers on arriving in Brighton would head for the pubs. At one time there were 110 public houses within half a mile of the Palace Pier.

Piermaster Weeks congratulating heavyweight boxer Jack Pettifer on getting a title fight fixed with Jack Doyle, 6 September 1932. A training area was used at the pier head with the spectators taking a keen interest in the action.

Jack Pettifer helps judge the Children's Beauty Competition on Saturday 27 August 1932. No doubt it was a difficult decision to make. During that season 'Professor' Zeilder was employed to laugh outside Laughter Land which we now know as the Hall of Mirrors, admission to which was 2*d*. He was subsequently replaced by a recording, an instance of technology taking over from man.

Holiday Kiddies Joy Day. Sunshine smiles and cheers on the Palace Pier as the Piermaster announces the first and second prize winners in the Children's Fancy Dress Contest at the carnival of 13 August 1932. Parents had put a lot of hard work into making costumes.

A hearty reception was given to a German girl canoeist, Fraulein Fridel Mayer, on Saturday 4 August 1934. Her frail craft, called the *Stella Maris*, flew the German flag and on board she had her pet Chow dog. A speed-boat was dispatched from the pier to escort her. Although her little craft was tossed perilously about by the waves, she showed an astonishing sense of balance. On arriving at the pier, she was served hot milk in the café. The final outcome of her adventure was never recorded.

Delightful photographic advertising card, 'You're All Cod'. The setting is underneath the pier.

All aboard for a speed-boat ride, Palace Pier, August 1935. Irish heavyweight boxer Jack Doyle (back right) with Charlie Searle. Born in August 1913, Doyle became one of the most colourful of all modern heavyweight boxers. He lost only four out of his nineteen fights; twelve of his wins were by knock-out. In 1938 he moved to the United States where in the course of his career he became a crooner, film actor and a variety star.

Little Man's Big Punch, c. 1936. The Cambridge boat race crew spent the weekend at Brighton. The cox, J.N. Duckworth, showed his strength on an Ahrens Punchball Machine, which cost 1d a go. He was also the only one to make a catch in a fishing competition.

Bathing Belles finalists awaiting adjudication during the Palace Pier Carnival on 8 August 1936. This was the first official Miss Brighton competition. On a fashion note, the third girl from the right is pioneering an early version of the bikini. 18,332 people passed through the pier turnstiles on that day.

Mrs D. Crane, extreme left, and family promenading on the Palace Pier 1937. Dorothy Crane and her late husband, Harold, moved to Brighton during August 1936 and lived at Guildford Street when they were first married. Harold worked as a painter and decorator. She has many vivid memories of the pier including dancing at the pier head and visits to the theatre to watch variety shows. 'Twice a week I would push my baby son, Raymond, along the deck. Some days it was so busy we had to go up the left-hand side and down the right.' They moved from Brighton during 1943 when the whole of the south coast was under threat of invasion and finally settled in Sutton, Surrey. Their four-year-old child, Raymond, was evacuated to an aunt in Yorkshire.

Front cover of a theatre programme, 1937. It epitomizes the fashion of the 1930s. During 1933 Prince George (1902–42), who became Duke of Kent in 1934, paid an unofficial visit to the Palace Pier. His party, including his Alsatian dog, enjoyed lunch at the Royal Albion Hotel with Mr Harry Preston. They went on to play the amusement machines on the pier. According to the reports in the local newspapers he played an array of penny-in-the-slot machines, including football, shooting and bicycle racing machines. He had his fortune told by a mechanical figure of Old Mother Shipton, who appeared from a cave to gaze into a crystal ball; this caused great amusement. Prince George had officiated at the opening of the redesigned aquarium in April 1930. He married Princess Marina of Greece and Denmark in 1934 and was killed in an air crash on active service with the RAF in Scotland in 1942.

Sitting with Piermaster Weeks is Haile Selassie, the Lion of Judah (1891–1975). This photograph was taken on a chilly April morning in 1937. Haile Selassie was Emperor of Ethiopia from 1930 to 1974, his country was invaded by Italy in 1935–6, and he lived in exile at Bath in England until 1941, when he was restored to the throne after liberation of his country by British forces. He was finally deposed by a military coup and died in mysterious circumstances in captivity. Piermaster Weeks recalled lending the Emperor an overcoat; 'he was a very sad man who at the time could not come to terms with what had happened in his country.' Rastafarians believe that he was the Messiah, the incarnation of God (Jah). One wonders whether he had to pay 2d for the deckchair hire!

Mr Oliver Dalton (1879–1939) was the Managing Director of the Brighton Marine Palace Pier Co. until his tragic death by suicide in October 1939. His early life was very much centred on the area of the seafront where the Palace Pier now stands. His widowed mother lived in Camelford Street near the Old Chain Pier. As a boy he must have witnessed the beginnings of the Palace Pier which would have seemed like an incredible engineering achievement. At the age of thirteen he unsuccessfully applied for a job on the pier as a time-keeper. Following service with the Imperial Yeomanry he returned from the Boer War to settle in Brighton. He was quick to see the opportunities as a bathing hut proprietor and gradually took his first steps up the ladder of commerce. According to his obituary in the *Herald* newspaper of 26 October 1939, his interests expanded into automatic machines and it was not long before this brought him his fortune. He eventually joined the board and acquired the controlling interest in the Palace Pier. He was an entrepreneur of mass culture but also saw the need to put money into essential maintenance work and expansion of facilities. His legacy included conservation work, notably the re-siting of the toll houses from the Chain Pier. One of these was rescued from nearby Queen's Park where it was being used as a garden shed. He made several visits to Atlantic City, USA, during the mid-1930s and drew inspiration from the experience to introduce Brighton's big wheel, dodgem car track and multi-coloured sea fountain, which operated to music. He catered for the amusement of thousands of holidaymakers. His wealth became enormous, but fate which so generously smiled on his business endeavours dealt him a cruel blow in his personal life: one of his five sons was killed in a car crash. The outbreak of the Second World War and the apparent loss of his business empire no doubt played an important part in his mental breakdown. After his death his wife Winifred became chairman of the board and took control of the company up to her retirement in 1973. She died on 27 November 1974.

Front cover of a theatre programme, 1935. The 28-seater charabancs can be seen lined up outside the pier after delivering day-trippers. Between the wars charabancs were used to transport visitors on outings. The Bristol Omnibus Company first introduced the motor coach in 1907. The speed limit in 1909 was only 12 mph, a slow journey to the coast. According to Alan Delgado, in his book *The Annual Outing & Other Excursions*, the charabancs had important advantages over the train: 'You can stop where you like to admire the scenery or call for refreshments.' The patrons were pampered with sprung seating, travelling rugs, illustrated guides and 'Cape Cart Hoods' for showery weather. Among the social traditions of charabanc outings were 'booze-ups': the vehicles were well stocked with bottled beer. Music was also an important ritual of the journey, with singing accompanied by a banjo, ukulele or squeeze-box.

Almost opposite the Palace Pier is the aquarium which was designed by Eugenius Birch who also built the West Pier. Opened in August 1872 the original 90-ft tank held over 2,500 gallons of water and a variety of sea life. In 1929, during the aquarium's reconstruction, the original clock tower was purchased by Oliver Dalton and moved to the entrance of the Palace Pier.

Holidaymakers enjoy the new thrill of the giant wheel at the end of the Palace Pier, 18 April 1938. Piermaster Weeks informed the *Evening Argus* that the Big Wheel had carried over 3,000 passengers on one single day during the Whitsun holiday. The Ferris Wheel originated in America and was designed by engineer George W.G. Ferris of Pittsburgh.

A book of twelve admission tickets costing 2s, c. 1939.

Taking tea in the café situated above the theatre entrance, 12 August 1939. The panoramic views of Brighton with 'teas at popular prices' must have been a great attraction.

Landlady of "Seaview." "YOU LEFT BOOKING RATHER LATE THIS YEAR, SIR. STILL, I WAS DETERMINED TO OBLIGE YOU, SO I SUBLET YOU TO SLEEP AT MRS. WIGGINS'S OVER BY THE GASWORKS, AND TO HAVE YOUR MEALS AT CREST VILLA, WHICH IS A MERE FIFTEEN MINUTES' WALK UP STEEPSIDE AVENUE."

Seaview Boarding Establishment with a saucy girl at the window almost beckoning visitors to step inside, *Punch*, 27 June 1934. This David Ghilchik cartoon, with a popular perennial landlady joke, shows the Palace Pier clocktower in the distance. David Ghilchik (1892–1972) was born in Romania but his family settled in England when he was five years of age. He trained at the Manchester School of Art and at the Slade School. His connection with *Punch* started when he wrote home from the First World War trenches sending illustrated letters depicting the 'lighter side of army life'. He worked for *Punch* for almost twenty years and his work was exhibited at the Royal Academy.

CHAPTER SIX

STEAMBOATS

To many the pier was essentially a tool in the hazardous task of landing waterborne passengers which required specific maritime skills and, in choppy seas, sober judgement. The replacement of wind power with steam engines had become a feature of shipping in the early nineteenth century and in the watercolour paintings of J.M.W. Turner and William Callow these new vessels were depicted as man's conquest over the forces of nature in the waters around the British Isles. However, steam's conquest of sail was not rapid and at the beginning of the twentieth century it was only just winning on the long-distance runs to the Far East and Australia. Steamboats, whether they had rotating paddles or were screw-driven, initially had engines that were too small to travel far without regular coaling stations, which confined them to the coastal waters of Europe and North America. They were unable to compete against the large-sailed clippers that could benefit from the Roaring Forties which constantly blew from west to east around the southern hemisphere and that, without fuel, had more room for cargo.

Whatever the drawbacks of steam on the greater oceans it had long been the driving force for passenger ferries to and from continental Europe, not least because the reliability of the services meant they could meet scheduled boat-trains from the ports to inland cities. Since the eighteenth century holidaymakers had been taken by sailing boats from London to such resorts as Southend-on-Sea, Gravesend and Ramsgate for weekend or longer trips. Paddle-steamers were so well established on these routes by the middle of the nineteenth century that they were able to compete with the railways during the summer months for the passage of holidaymakers.

The location of Brighton on the south coast gave the railways an advantage for passengers from London, but for those with sufficient time and money a sea-trip could be made by paddle-steamer from London's Tower Pier to Ramsgate and, by changing boats when and where necessary along the south coast, to Cornwall and around into the Bristol Channel.

The coast of East Anglia, the south and south-west of England, the Low Countries and Northern France were served by steamers across the North Sea and the English

Channel, and between resorts along the same coastline. The whole system worked in much the same manner as the *vaporetti* that take passengers around the canals and the lagoons of Venice, but on a much larger and more complex scale. The pleasure element of those steamers was evident in the names that were given to them, such as the *Sussex Belle*, the *Plymouth Belle* and the *Brighton Queen* before the First World War. The few that were still usable after the war were joined in the 1920s and 1930s by the *Lady Moyra* – later renamed the *Brighton Belle* – the *Glen Gower*, the *Empress Queen*, the *Worthing Belle* and the *Devonia*, among many others of that period.

The Palace Pier offered regular services to the inter-resort traffic and to passengers bound for France. The *Worthing Belle* offered 'popular trips' to and from Newhaven, Worthing and Littlehampton at 'popular fares' of 1s 6d first class and 1s second class – 7½ and 5 new pence respectively. Prominent among the companies which owned and operated the steamships were P. & A. Campbell, Cosens and the Southampton Company. The Southern Railway also became involved in order to participate in the traffic to Dieppe. The railway company's shipping could sail from either the Palace Pier or from the docks further east at Newhaven.

For the crews the hours of work were long and the pay modest to say the least as their own meals and accommodation were taken into account. An ordinary seaman's wages were well below £2 a week in the 1920s and girls, who were employed to run the refreshment room, look after the lady passengers and to keep the cabins tidy, received less than £1 for equally long and unsociable hours.

Mrs L.V. Martin of Gravesend, Kent, remembers working on the *Worthing Belle*, serving refreshments and carrying out general cleaning duties during the late 1930s. She said that the duties 'although poorly paid for the hours worked were a better alternative for a young girl than going into service during those years'. Shop work was difficult to obtain and fiercely competed for in her home-town of Eastbourne, whereas 'working upon the ferries provided regular employment that, although it was away from home was known to be well regulated and well chaperoned . . . in other words was seen as "respectable" by the neighbours. It also made my transference to the Women's Royal Naval Service during the war much easier to cope with.'

Between the wars some of the inter-resort traffic was taken by charabancs which were the preferred transport option for those who were prone to sea-sickness. The Second World War took its toll on the steamers; the *Brighton Queen*, the *Brighton Belle* and the *Devonia* were lost during the Dunkirk evacuation and others were mined or sunk in port during air raids. What vessels remained of the fleet were used for pleasure craft during the 'austerity years' after 1945, but by the early 1960s the demand for larger cross-Channel ferries to carry cars and lorries and the growth of package tour holidays to the Mediterranean made what was left obsolete.

P. & A. CAMPBELL LTD.

SPITHEAD.

THE GREAT ASSEMBLY OF
250 WAR VESSELS.

MAGNIFICENT ILLUMINATIONS
AND SEARCHLIGHT DISPLAY

IN THE EVENING.

SPECIAL AFTERNOON & EVENING EXCURSIONS

BY THE CROSS CHANNEL STEAMERS,

DEVONIA & BRIGHTON BELLE

Well equipped with fine Saloons, and Catering a speciality.

SATURDAY, JULY 26th

The "BRIGHTON BELLE" leaves Brighton Palace Pier 2.45 p.m., West Pier 3 p.m. for a Cruise through the various lines of Warships, afterwards takes up her position to witness the Illuminations, then returning to Brighton. Back about 2 a.m.

Tickets obtained before the day, 8/6 ; on the day, 10/6.

From Messrs. THOS. COOK & SON, 81, King's Road. Brighton, or at the Company's Office, 7, Old Steine, Brighton.

SATURDAY, JULY 26th

Evening Trip to Spithead to View the Illuminations.

The "DEVONIA" leaves Brighton Palace Pier 6.50 p.m., West Pier 7 p.m. and takes up her position in time to see the Marvellous Exhibition of 250 War Vessels Illuminated, then returning to Brighton. Back about 1.30 a.m. Fare 5/-

Full particulars may be obtained from P. & A. CAMPBELL Ltd., 7, Old Steine, Brighton. W. REID, Agent.

The Southern Publishing Co., Ltd., 130, North Street, Brighton. P984.

The coronation of King Edward VII was to have taken place on 28 June 1902. A few days before the coronation the King was taken ill with appendicitis and the Naval Review was postponed. The King made a speedy recovery and the event took place on 16 August 1902.

Passengers on the deck of the paddle-steamer *Brighton*, *c*. 1902. Constructed of wood by Johnson of North Shields in 1893, she was 105 ft long and weighed 100 tons. She ended her days at Shoreham Harbour where she was burnt out in 1904.

Paddle-steamer *Brighton Queen* looking fully laden with passengers on deck, *c*. 1910. Constructed of steel at Clydebank by S.B. & Co. Ltd in 1897, she was 240 ft long and weighed 553 gross tons. A great deal of thought went into satisfying passengers' needs. The onboard facilities included music and dancing; various stalls offered books and fruit and special attention was paid to catering. During the First World War many steamers were requisitioned by the Royal Navy and used as minesweepers. The *Brighton Queen* was lost in 1915 while on minesweeping duties.

Hand-tinted postcard showing a Red Funnel paddle-steamer departing from the Palace Pier, 1910. There was excessive competition and rivalry between the paddle-steamer operators for a slice of trade during the restricted season.

Paddle-steamer *Glen Rosa*, 28 March 1910. She operated at Brighton from 1903. Constructed by Caird & Co., she was 206 ft in length and 296 gross tons. The *Glen Rosa* was scrapped in 1919. It is interesting to note that the London, Brighton & South Coast Railway obtained parliamentary permission in 1912 to run from the Palace Pier to Dieppe. This was a weekly service with passengers returning to Newhaven.

The crew of the paddle-steamer *Waverley*, c. 1927. This delightful photographic postcard shows the entire crew assembled on deck of the vessel as she lies next to the Palace Pier. There have been a number of paddle-steamers named the *Waverley*; this vessel was formerly called the *Barry* and started work on the Brighton coast during Easter 1926. Captain Weeks (centre above the lifebelt) joined P. & A. Campbell's of Bristol during 1922. The dining-room on board the *Waverley* was described as 'lofty and airy' and was fitted with electric fans. She could carry well over 800 passengers. Built by Messrs John Brown & Co. Ltd of Clydebank, Scotland, in 1907, she had a bridge deck for passengers amidships, with a ticket office and wireless cabin underneath. She was 225 ft long and weighed 471 tons gross. Paddle-steamers always offered good value for money for passengers but for the crew life was hard. The steward wearing a white jacket appears to have a black eye. Occasionally hours were long but when a vessel lay at anchor a sing-song would be organized. The *Waverley* was lost during the Second World War when she was bombed in 1941. The ship's mascot was a doll with a feather headdress.

Captain Frederick Weeks with his wife Ada and son Alan (aged four), sitting on deck of the paddle-steamer *Waverley*, next to the white funnel, 1928. Top right can be seen the skee ball stall, a forerunner of today's bowling alleys. It was in this year that Captain Weeks joined the Palace Pier staff as Piermaster and remained in post until 1955, twenty-seven years of service. Prior to this he had spent twenty-five years at sea, rising from deckhand to skipper and travelling the world. After the First World War he became skipper of P. & A. Campbell's paddle-steamers *Ravenswood* and the *Waverley*. He was employed as Piermaster by Oliver Dalton no doubt because his nautical skills were very useful when ships were being tied to the pier. He wore a gold-braided uniform with three rings on his sleeve and a row of war ribbons on his chest. The men under his command were known as the crew and he was referred to as the 'skipper'. They worked watches and spoke about 'going ashore'. The Palace Pier was a self-contained industry; it had a summer staff of 300 including its own blacksmith, carpenters, electricians, plumbers, restaurant staff and a resident diver to check the underwater structure. Captain Weeks kept a piermaster's logbook, recording nautical matters and other events. Over the years he met a number of distinguished visitors including Emperor Haile Selassie, Prince George (later Duke of Kent), Bette Davis, Amy Johnson, and many sporting personalities such as Jack Pettifer and Jack Doyle. In 1950 he described his job as 'controlling the traffic, the visitors, the steam passengers, lost property, lost children, and taking fish hooks out of people'. He was very fond of watching ice hockey. His son, Alan, became a household name as the golden voice of television's ice skating with the BBC. Alan Weeks sadly died on 11 June 1996.

A visiting paddle-steamer captain with Oliver Dalton (centre) and Captain F. Weeks (right), *c.* 1930. The revenue arising from the landing of steam boats was important to the pier owners.

Southern and Great Western Railways and P. & A. Campbell Ltd.

SPECIAL EXCURSION

From Brighton, Worthing, Eastbourne & Hastings

TO ILFRACOMBE, CARDIFF & BRISTOL

(Weather and circumstances permitting), by the Magnificent Saloon Steamer

"DEVONIA"

On Thursday, Sept. 29th, 1927

Leaving BRIGHTON (Palace Pier) at 11.30 a.m., due to arrive at Ilfracombe about noon on Friday, Sept. 30th, leaving 4.30 p.m for Cardiff, arrive 7.0 p.m., Bristol about 8.45 p.m.

Single Fare for the Steamer 15/- (Tickets on Board).

Return Fares to ILFRACOMBE, CARDIFF, BRISTOL

					OUT BY BOAT HOME BY RAIL
From	**BRIGHTON**	40/-	35/-	30/-	Passengers from
,,	**WORTHING**	40/-	36/6	31/-	Worthing, Eastbourne and Hastings join the
,,	**EASTBOURNE**	49/6	42/-	37/-	Steamer at Brighton
,,	**HASTINGS**	51/6	44/6	40/-	Palace Pier.

The journeys from Bristol and Cardiff to Brighton may be made either via London or Salisbury. From Ilfracombe by the Salisbury and Southern Co. route only. Those to Eastbourne and Hastings via London only. Those to Worthing via the Salisbury and Southern Co. route only.

Tickets may be obtained in advance from Messrs. T. Cook & Son, 81 King's Rd., Brighton, or at the Southern Railway Company's Booking Offices, Brighton, Worthing, Eastbourne and Hastings, available to return by any train carrying third-class passengers, up to and including October 16th by the routes specified above.

Full particulars from Agents of P. & A. CAMPBELL Ltd.

W. REID, 15 Ship Street, Brighton.   Telegrams : "Ravenswood, Brighton."   Telephone : 5478 Brighton.
W. A. PELLY, Pier, Eastbourne.   Telegrams : "Pier, Eastbourne."   Telephone : 1690 Eastbourne.
F. L. PHILLIPS, Pier, Hastings.   Telegrams : "Pier, Hastings."   Telephone : 1032 Hastings.

| 2003 | **BRIGHTON & SOUTH COAST STEAMERS LTD.** | 2003 | 2002 | **BRIGHTON & SOUTH COAST STEAMERS LTD.** | 2002 |

BRIGHTON & SOUTH COAST
STEAMERS LTD.
2003   2003

Brighton to
WORDING
Fare as Advertised

Issued subject to conditions as
stated in the Company's Time
Tables and Bills.

BRIGHTON & SOUTH COAST
STEAMERS LTD.
2002   2002

Brighton to
WORTHING
Fare as Advertised

Issued subject to conditions as
stated in the Company's Time
Tables and Bills.

The cheapest and most frequent steamboat service was to Worthing. Typical fares during the 1920s were 1s 6d first class and 1s second class, the journey lasting no more than one hour.

A Campbell's paddle-steamer coming into land at the Palace Pier, c. 1930. This was the tricky part of the operation and was overseen by the piermaster; no major accidents were recorded. According to the by-laws of 1911, if a red flag was flying from the signal yard at the pier head by day, or two red lights were placed in a vertical position (4 ft apart) at night, no steamer could be brought alongside the pier.

The paddle-steamer *Gracie Fields* was launched on 8 April 1936 by the radio and film star whose name she bore. This postcard was sent by Captain N.R. Larkin to crew member Mr William Ranger who was unwell. Built at Thornycroft's, Southampton, the paddle-steamer weighed 393 gross tons and was capable of a speed of 14 knots, being intended for an all-year service between Southampton and Cowes, Isle of Wight. During 1936 she sailed from Southampton to Brighton's Palace Pier to give a cruise to children from a Peacehaven orphanage of which Gracie Fields was the patron. The vessel was sunk at Dunkirk on 29 May 1940 during the famous evacuation from France. She had 750 soldiers on board when she was hit by German aircraft.

Captain F.C. Weeks (left) and Walley Stuart, Assistant Deputy Piermaster, steady the gangway in readiness for the arrival of passengers from a pleasure steamer during August 1949. Each vessel had to disembark passengers within fifteen minutes. The master of each paddle-steamer had to make sure that 'fires shall not be stoked as to cause smoke while the vessel is lying alongside the Pier'.

Holidaymakers form an orderly queue for a trip on the magnificent turbine steamer *Empress Queen*, summer 1950. She was 282 ft in length and 1,781 gross tons, and was operated by P. & A. Campbell of Bristol – the company's fleet was popularly known as 'The White Funnel Fleet'. She was ordered in 1939 from the Ailsa Shipbuilding Co. of Troon and her engines were made by Harland & Wolff of Belfast. Delivered in 1940, she could carry 1,000 passengers. During the Second World War she saw action as a floating anti-aircraft battery. Her draught and size limited the number of piers that she could call at. The season of 1950 was a poor one commercially, which is hard to imagine looking at this busy photograph. The *Empress Queen* proved unsuitable for short trips and was withdrawn and moved to Torquay. It was a sad day when she left Bristol for the last time on 3 April 1955, her destination being Greece where she was renamed *Philippos*. Top right in this photograph are the railings of the Tea Garden which finished trading at the end of the 1939 season. The advert for the dodgem cars must have been tempting, promising lots of thrills and spills.

P. & A. Campbell's steamer *Glen Gower* was the sole operator at Brighton during 1954, 16,000 passengers being carried that year. The 'no passport' trips were very popular.

CHAPTER SEVEN

SECOND WORLD WAR

The pier's abrupt closure in May 1940 was followed by years when national security was regarded as more important than holidays and visitors to Brighton were not only discouraged but also eyed with suspicion. All piers and jetties were seen by the War Office as potentially useful to sea-borne invasion forces, and in order to render the structure harmless a section of the Palace Pier was removed; the remainder was as heavily mined as the beach beneath it.

Neither of these measures was a response to ill-founded alarmist speculation since Brighton's position on the south-east coast did indeed make it vulnerable after the evacuation from Dunkirk to enemy invasion. If such an invasion had occurred in this vicinity the town would almost certainly have been badly damaged if not entirely destroyed. To get some idea of what this would have meant, a visit to modern Ostend, Calais or Plymouth shows what once proud resorts and ports are reduced to without their fine pre-war buildings.

The Luftwaffe, however, did inflict considerable damage upon Brighton with fifty-six raids that killed more than 200 people and injured many more. Most of the attacks were sporadic hit-and-run raids which destroyed or seriously damaged more than 1,000 buildings. The Kemp Town district was badly hit and the bombs around the Stein came close to destroying the Royal Pavilion. The prominent Palace Pier must have presented a tempting target for German bombers and, although it was not destroyed, the East Pavilion Sun Terrace was badly damaged by shrapnel. The accidental explosion of a beach mine caused extensive damage to the clock tower and its surrounding structures at the pier's entrance in 1941.

In addition to the damage by enemy and 'friendly' fire, greater havoc was wreaked simply by the sheer neglect of the pier during the war years. The lack of paint on its woodwork left it exposed to the rotting effects of the elements, and the rust attacking so much of its ironwork must have been almost irreversible after five years. However, late in the summer of 1945 the missing sections were replaced and work began on the clearing of mines on and under the pier. Years of austerity lay ahead for the British, but to local people and visitors the pier's re-opening in 1946 was seen as one small step to the 'normality' of pre-war times. After nearly six years of warfare, divided families, air raids, blackouts and rationing, the unemployment and poverty that many had suffered in the 1930s tended to be forgotten and, even if rationing was still around, the future seemed bright.

Home Guard beach patrol, October 1939. Bewildered holidaymakers watch as the beach is patrolled. As the retreat from Dunkirk unfolded on the evening of Thursday 23 May 1940, without any warning the pier was requisitioned and the theatre closed. A performance of *The First Mrs Fraser* was about to begin with the audience already assembled. A full refund had to be given as the audience filed out. There were no further performances until after hostilities had ceased. The beaches were eventually mined, the sea front was heavily guarded and many anti-aircraft batteries were set up. In August 1940 the German planners of 'Operation Sealion' (the invasion of England) planned to land between 4,000 and 5,000 men at Brighton from motor-boats. By September 12 per cent of Hitler's invasion transport had been destroyed by the RAF. The invasion plan was postponed until the spring of 1941; instead Hitler turned his attention to the ill-fated invasion of Russia. Plans for the invasion of England were accordingly shelved.

This photograph was taken during 1939 when there were appeals for scrap metal to help the war effort. The Palace Pier disposed of a number of spare piles, each weighing 3 tons. The company involved in carrying out the removal to a British foundry was Messrs M. Freeman & Co. A stark reminder of the horror of the First World War can be seen advertised on the Old Chain Pier toll booth – 'Every article on this side was made by limbless ex-servicemen.'

Photographic postcard dated 15 March 1940, from Mr E. Thomas 960760 'C' Battery, 'G' Troop, No. 2 Squadron, 41st Survey Training Regiment, R.A. Preston Barracks, Brighton, to his cousin, Lil Groom of Bridgend, Glamorgan, South Wales.

The Palace Pier was cut in half and heavily mined for the duration of the war. The breaching of the pier was carried out by sappers from the Royal Engineers in May 1940. The team was led by Captain Peter Fleming, assisted by Captain M. Calverl (known as 'Mad Mike'), and the gap they created was 40 ft wide. A secret War Office paper identified the possible direction and scale of a German invasion. Admiral Sir Frederick C. Dreyer recommended that the majority of piers around the country should have three spans removed to prevent the passage of troops and light infantry vehicles. The pier was not repaired until September 1945, four months after VE Day. It reopened on 6 June 1946.

View from Madeira Drive towards the breached Palace Pier, 1940. Up until the surrender of France on 20 June 1940 the reality of the war had not fully hit home. But then the atmosphere in Brighton changed overnight as barbed wire was uncoiled and naval guns were installed on cliffs. The sobering truth of war was beginning to unfold.

A Hotchkis heavy machine-gun, which fired .303 ammunition, being assembled on the roof of the Palace Pier Theatre, *c.* 1940. During the war years all the amusement machines were removed from the pier and stored in a garage in George Street, Brighton, for safety.

The barbed-wire entanglements stretch between the two piers along the barricaded promenade. At 11.17 a.m. on Sunday 3 September 1939 the war's first air-raid warning wailed out over Brighton. The event was a false alarm but it stirred Brighton into the full reality of war. According to Ernest A. Hawkins, in his book *Brighton (& Sussex) at War 1939–1945*, 'inside Brighton a dusk till dawn curfew was imposed on all residents living inside an area roughly 300 yards north of the front'.

Brighton front by moonlight. This is a time exposure photograph taken while the curfew was in operation. The streaks of white are the lights from military vehicles.

The Palace Pier clock in a sorry state. The clock mechanism had been removed for safety. The clock itself suffered damage from an explosion of beach mines in 1941.

This rare aerial photograph was taken by the Germans during 1944. It shows clearly the breaches in the Palace and West Piers. The camera used was remote controlled. At the top right can be seen the shadow of an aircraft fin which may have been from a Dornier 17 or 217 which were used for strategic reconnaissance. Apparently suitable landing spots for paratroopers had been identified on the South Downs behind the town.

Although German dive bombers made frequent attempts to destroy the pier, only near misses were registered. This photograph shows shrapnel damage to the East Pavilion sun terrace. There was a constant threat of attack from 'sneak' aircraft flying across the Channel.

The first raid on Brighton was at 6 a.m. on 15 July 1940 by a single German raider on Kemp Town. Hitler's proud boast that he would be living in the Prince Regent's Royal Palace before the end of 1940 was no more than pie in the sky rhetoric. This picture shows Douglas Boston IIIs of 226 Squadron escorted probably by Spitfire Vs.

Sappers using an Aural mine detector search for unaccounted beach mines east of the Palace Pier, 1945. Not a job for the faint hearted!

A bulldozer levelling off heaps of shingle to allow the mine detectors to reach the required depth.

Evening photograph of Madeira Drive, *c.* 1945. All the barbed-wire entanglements have now been removed and the seafront returns to normal. In the distance the breach of the Palace Pier is still visible. The Brighton Marine Palace Pier Co. received compensation from the government following the Second World War to cover the damage done during the breaching.

CHAPTER EIGHT

THE POSTWAR YEARS

The years that followed the austerity of the 1940s witnessed a general increase in the standard of living throughout the country. The rationing of food and clothing eventually ended, full employment was taken for granted in most regions and, allowing for some exceptions in the north, Harold Macmillan's 1959 claim that 'you've never had it so good' was true for most people. International confidence in the pound sterling meant it still bought eight German marks in the early 1960s which, together with higher wages and secure employment, allowed more people to holiday abroad. If English resorts in general suffered from these trends, Brighton's long relationship with the short-stay visitor made it less vulnerable to such changes.

Not all visitors were welcomed in the 1960s when the resort, and even the piers, became the battleground for the Mods and Rockers during weekends and Bank Holidays. Arriving on their motorbikes and scooters, which gave them a mobility that few police vehicles could match, these twentieth-century imitators of the Goths and Huns fought running battles along the seafront between themselves, with the police or with anyone else who challenged them. They may have been outnumbered by the gentlemen of the press who faithfully recorded the proceedings on camera for the newspapers and television, accounts which in turn were read or watched by a public comforted by the thought of its own moral superiority.

The increased spending power of visitors accelerated a process of social change and new fashion demonstrated by women's clothes, or lack of them, in the form of mini-skirts and hot-pants. Men's fashions changed as well and the once obligatory suit or jacket, worn with a tie, gave way to jeans and open shirts in bright colours that had not been seen on men since the early nineteenth century. The legalization of Brighton's nudist beach in 1980 provides some measurement of the social changes that had taken place since the Palace Pier was first opened.

What visitors bought and how they amused themselves on the Palace Pier also changed with the times. The traditional fast food in the form of fish and chips was challenged to some extent by American hot-dogs and hamburgers. Many of the traditional machines and games that were mechanically driven gave way in the 1980s to electronic ones that began with 'Space Invaders' and went on to develop the concept of virtual reality. These electronic innovations were, for the most part, the preserve of the young, but it might have passed the minds of more mature observers, who were either afraid or bewildered by the new machines, that it was something of a contradiction to pay for reality, in the virtual or any other form, in the very place that had offered an escape from it for most of the century.

Graham Greene's best-seller, *Brighton Rock*, which centred on gang life in Brighton, was shot on the Palace Pier in the summer of 1947. It was directed by John Boulting (shirtless on camera dolly). The cast included Sir Richard Attenborough as Pinkie Brown and Carol Marsh as Rose. Other actors included Hermione Baddeley and William Hartnell. It was a film which in retrospect did not advertise Brighton in a good light, perpetuating the gang-war image of that time.

Three men in a boat, *c.* 1950. Pictured left to right are Gus Ingle (foreman), Mr Hards (pier engineer) and Mr Kennard (deckhand) on an inspection mission. They were looking for broken ties or damage to lattice girders. A 2-lb hammer would be used to chip away at rust to expose good metalwork. Once a year Mr Mason, an outside structural engineer, would undertake a complete check. It was this dedication to maintenance that enabled the Palace Pier to survive.

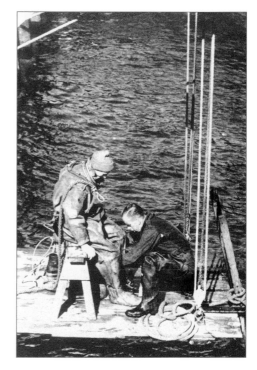

Diver Arthur Cowley sitting on a raft preparing to dive, *c.* 1950. His assistant is fitting weighted lead boots. No underwater welding was done but cutting was undertaken. The visibility underwater was often poor when divers were searching for visible damage that was mostly caused by the abrasive tidal action of the sand. Metal collars would be clamped on to the piles as an essential method of repair.

Arthur Cowley descends slowly, *c.* 1950. Divers would have to be patient until underwater visibility had cleared; sometimes this could take weeks.

Arthur Cowley with mate Ted Lane, holding the block and tackle, preparing for an inspection dive, *c.* 1950s. Divers were superstitious and liked to work with the same partners. Luckily on the Palace Pier no major accidents were recorded, merely a few minor knocks and bruises.

Presenting the trophy for the popular *News of the World* fishing competition, 1950s. Left to right: actor Leslie Holmes, General Manager Walter Fern, Piermaster Captain F. Weeks and the winning fisherman.

Foreman Gus Ingle (pictured centre) with two younger colleagues taking a dismantled stall back to their workshop, *c*.1950. Everything was moved around on trolleys in order to protect the decking.

Archery competition taking place at the pier head, *c.* 1950. As well as flying flags, the mast pictured centre was used for signal purposes to inform paddle-steamers where to berth. By exhibiting a ball cone it would indicate that the lee side should be used for berthing and a diamond signal indicated the weather side. No vessel other than passenger paddle-steamers with a gross tonnage not exceeding 1,000 tons were allowed to make fast. The mast used for signals stood 93 ft high.

Palace of Fun, 1950. Nightwatchman Jacob Phillis is sweeping up after 20,000 visitors. The interior shows left to right the skee ball machine, Kentucky Derby and the Rollo Stall, better known today as Bingo. Jean Penny of Brighton, whose father was Thomas Meiklejohn, a director of the Palace Pier during the 1930s, recalls the restrictions on gambling prior to the Casino Act of the early 1970s: 'The joints (stalls) gave away prizes such as "Festival Glass", a cheap orange glassware.' This is now better known as Carnival Glass and has, surprisingly, become a collector's item.

Evening photograph taken looking down the deck from the theatre on the west side. The boxing punch balls are lined up (left) no doubt so that young men could impress the young ladies with feats of strength.

Early morning finds a group of beachcombers working in a line under the Palace Pier, 1952. The process was also known as 'blacksanding'. The equinoctial tides would shift tons of shingle to reveal the gratton where hidden treasures such as coins and jewellery might be found.

Brighton Pier, 1958. This linocut by Edward Bawden (1903–89) was printed in six colours in an edition of fifty. According to David Beevers in his book *Brighton Revealed through Artists' Eyes, c. 1760–1960* Bawden worked in a 'realist tradition' and never specialized in one medium. This linocut shows the pier flanked on one side by the domes of the Royal Pavilion and on the other by late Regency houses.

Pier Head, *c.* 1962. Walter Fern is announcing the Rod of the Week fishing competition winners. The youngsters in the front row look on anxiously for the result. Fern was General Manager from 1947 to his death in 1969. His background before joining the pier was in the theatre; he worked with the Bing Boys and then became an entertainment officer.

Janet Patterson, on holiday from Hawick, Scotland, poses for a photograph at the pier entrance, 1965. The use of animals in photography has now become politically incorrect. The hard-sell tactics of beach photographers always left one with the fear that there was no film in the camera.

Palmist Madame Binney, pictured inside her stall, was concentrating hard, taking part in a documentary film in 1966. Rumour had it that she had a trap-door under her stall, located on the west side of the theatre, which she used to fish from.

Part of the 1969 film *Oh What A Lovely War* was shot in the Palace Pier Theatre. This photograph shows the set decorator at work; the backdrop is Roedean School with the wrought-iron school gates. Roedean School used to be described as the 'Eton of the fair sex'. It started life in a house in Lewis Crescent, Kemp Town, in 1885 and moved to its present-day on open land location on the outskirts of Brighton in 1899. The film was set in the First World War, directed by Richard Attenborough, and was an anti-war satirical entertainment with songs. The star-studded cast included Ralph Richardson, John Gielgud, Kenneth More, Jack Hawkins, Vanessa, Corin and Michael Redgrave, Maggie Smith, Nanette Newman, Dirk Bogarde, Edward Fox and Lawrence Olivier, to name but a few. Sir Lawrence Olivier's portrayal of Field Marshal Sir John French received critical acclaim and won him the British Academy award (BAFTA) for Best Supporting Actor.

The Grimaldi family pose for the camera after a visit to the Palace Pier, *c.* 1969. Left to right: Prince Rainier, Prince Albert, Princess Stephanie, Princess Grace and Princess Caroline. Princess Grace, former US film actress Grace Kelly, married Prince Rainier III in 1956.

Dick Philps pictured outside his Canadian waffle stall, *c.* 1969. The stall was situated to the east of the Palace of Fun entrance. Dick ran the stall with the help of his wife and sons up to March 1971. During the 1970s the pier housed over forty shops and outlets, the sale of food being especially popular. From candy floss to jellied eels, all tastes were catered for!

Kenneth Cope and Bernard Bresslaw taking advantage of a break in filming the British comedy farce *Carry On At Your Convenience* in 1979. Thirty-one *Carry On* films were made over two decades. This film was about the troubles at the factory of W.C. Boggs, played by Kenneth Williams, making toiletware. Shop Steward Vic Spanner (Sid James) clashes with Boggs and calls the workers out on strike. The cast also included Charles Hawtrey, Joan Sims, Hattie Jacques, Jacki Piper, Bill Maynard and Bill Pertwee. Directed by Gerald Thomas for Peter Rogers Productions, it was memorable among the *Carry On* films.

Fashion photograph taken during 1970 at the entrance to the Palace of Fun where the Mutoscopes were located. The style of boots shown is fashionable again today.

Staff from the Palace of Fun larking around, *c.* 1970.

Silhouette artist Arthur Forrester worked on the Palace
Pier from 1967 to 1972. He had a remarkable skill and
would cut the silhouette out in 'freehand' without
sketching in pencil. His son John followed the same
profession on the West Pier. These were skills that
Brighton had first seen demonstrated on the Old Chain
Pier during the 1860s.

Ted Lane, who was the pier plumber, takes a well-earned break on top of the Palace Pier Theatre roof, *c.* 1972. The panoramic view of Brighton was spectacular, and this was also a good spot to sunbathe and take the sea air.

Carpenters Ted Ford and Andy Brooks re-decking the area to the west of the theatre, 6 November 1972. During the 1970s about £100,000 a year was spent on maintenance work.

Hilda Everett, the General Manager's wife, presenting trophies to fishing competition winners, 1972. Left to right: Graham Manser, Senior Champion, Hilda Everett, Michael Arnold, Junior Champion, and Frank Vine, Club Secretary.

Sheikh Abdullah Jaber Al-Sabah, then ruler of Kuwait, promenading the deck, 1972. He owned a property overlooking the Brighton Marina and according to William Everett, the pier's General Manager, 'he would dispatch his bodyguard to secure a favourite bench in order to enjoy a particular view.' The Sheikh ruled until 1977 and was succeeded by his brother, Crown Prince Jabir, the present head of state.

The Mayor of Brighton, Councillor Danny Sheldon, inspects repair work to girders, *c.* 1974. He was accompanied by his wife Lilian and the Piermaster, Bill Brooks. Bill joined the company as an electrician in 1946 and was appointed Piermaster on 11 December 1972. He served until 1987. In the background, left to right, are Derek Martin, Company Chairman, William Everett, General Manager, and Dave Mannery, Archway Engineering.

The Palace Pier has been a popular subject for many artists and advertisers over the years, including those promoting the Palace Shell Fishbar, 1975.

The helter-skelter, which was demolished in 1973 following severe structural damage, was replaced in 1977. The replacement was purchased from Mr Taylor of Rhyl for £1,700, having been advertised in the *World Fair* magazine. On a clear day you can see the Isle of Wight from the top.

Artist David Peacock of Rotherfield produced this lively line drawing of the Palace Pier on 19 June 1979.

Alf Taylor and William Everett preparing for the Queen Elizabeth's Silver Jubilee celebrations of 1977. Relics of the 1953 coronation were discovered under the theatre stage and were spruced up. William Everett joined the Brighton Marina Palace Pier Co. in 1947 as a clerk. He was interviewed by Walter Fern and given the job on the understanding that he could type. His first salary was £5 a week. He eventually worked his way up to Chief Cashier and from 1969 to 1984 was General Manager.

A near miss! The Greek coaster *Athena B* embedded in the shingle of Brighton beach after having ran aground at 9.15 a.m. on 21 January 1980. In the foreground people gather to view the spectacle. The ship was finally pulled off in early February. Another 500 yards further and it would have caused serious damage to the Palace Pier.

The Red Arrows perform a 'Diamond Nine' over the Palace Pier, 16 May 1980. During the display one of the Hawker jets hit the top of a yacht's mast during a tricky manoeuvre. The mast was 43 ft high and the Pilot, Sqn Ldr Stephen Johnson, aged thirty-one, safely ejected and landed between the piers. Forty per cent of the remains of the shattered £1.5m Hawk was recovered from a depth of 15 ft. Although the area was sealed off, a sub-aqua diver was arrested within half an hour of the accident under the Official Secrets Act. The yacht was owned by Mr Marling, a County Court Registrar from East Farleigh, near Maidstone. Sqn Ldr Johnson suffered minor cuts and bruises after being blasted from the Hawk jet and was subsequently grounded for ten days. The plane could have easily crashed into the pier with a huge loss of life; a lucky escape indeed!

Pier staff gather around to see a cheque presented by Bonny Manzi in the centre and Alan Weeks front right, to the NSPCC, 14 November 1981. The charity event was a winkle-picking competition.

As a member of the maintenance staff Ted Lane pops up during a painting job on 8 September 1981 and is obviously impressed by what he sees! The two young ladies are enjoying ice-creams on this sunny day, but beware – there may be splinters in the decking.

Mr W. Everett, Manager of the Palace Pier, with a museum exhibit of diving equipment used for routine underwater inspections. The helmet and collar weighed 28 lb. The bulk of the early moving picture and animated model amusement machines behind were sold to a private British collector in 1972, following fierce competition from America.

A display of antiquated saucy photographs in machines made by the International Mutoscope Reel Co., USA. The photographs dated from about 1927 and their titles combined a mixture of violence and mildly erotic risqué scenes. They originated from Coney Island and were based on the silent movie principle.

Cheerful Toll Keeper, Arthur Rutter, hard at work in 1983. The toll for that year was only 20p.

Welcome to the World Famous Palace Pier Christmas decorations, 1986. The Noble Organization purchased the Grade II listed Pier in 1984 for £1½m. Following the demolition of the theatre in 1986 temporary permission was granted for a dome-shaped structure to be built on its site. The dome is 115 ft in diameter and 30 ft high. It provides a multipurpose space which is used as an amusement arcade with kiosks outside. This structure will have been removed by the year 2000 and replaced with a building similar to the Edwardian theatre, complete with colonnade and oriental domes. The Noble Organization has given the pier a new lease of life with an £8m refurbishment and enlargement plan.

The temptation to ignore the warning sign is too much for these young boys as they climb the lattice girders, 1986. Onlookers enjoy their dangerous exploits. This photograph is by John Hulme.

A youthful crowd gathers to witness a portrait artist at work, *c.* 1987. Judging by the quality of the work on display, his services were probably much in demand.

Virtual reality amusements inside the Palace of Fun, 1989. The stained-glass porthole windows surrounding the building have all been renovated to a very high standard. There are no longer any stalls in the Palace of Fun, the area being devoted to amusement machines. Plans for the pier's survival are now driven by hard economics rather than nostalgic optimism.

There is no better way to relax than enjoying a snooze in a deck-chair on the Palace Pier following in the footsteps of millions of holidaymakers, 6 August 1989. Deck-chairs originated on the Peninsular and Oriental Navigation Company liners going to India and the East.

A busker outside the Pier, 1989. Such informal entertainment remains popular today.

Digging for lug worms at the east of the Palace Pier, 28 April 1990. Following the pier's purchase by the Noble Organization in 1984, fishing from it was phased out. This eliminated any potential danger to promenaders from live casting and allowed the deck area at the pier head to be extended to accommodate further amusements.

This photograph was taken on a cold February day in 1990. A windscreen running down the centre of the deck was erected in 1906. The background view reveals a busy skyline; on the right can be seen the distinctive layered design of the American Express building based in Edward Street.

A test of strength, May 1990. Man against machine has long been a popular contest. With the early gripper machines used on the pier at the turn of the century a bell would ring whenever they were held firmly enough. It would be interesting to know on whom the model in this photograph was based.

This photograph, taken on 6 May 1990, is a fine example of the art of social documentary photography. Waitresses are taking a well-earned break outside the fish and chip restaurant. The building stands on the site of the original bandstand, the original supports of which can still be seen inside the building. The galleon weathervane spins in the wind above the mirror globe which sparkles and catches the eye from a distance. The aroma of a superb fish and chip meal intermingles with the salt-tanged air.

Clowns' Day, 3 July 1990, is an echo of the fairground link of yesteryear which has always existed on the pier. The Blessing of Rides is still done today, following the age-old fairground tradition.

Parents look on as children enjoy a ride on the stilt-walker's oversized scooter, July 1990.

The forecourt of the Palace Pier has always been a busy meeting area. Clowns' Day reveals the man on stilts charming the children, while another clown performs magic with sleight of hand.

We are not amused! Albert Bullock, co-author, and his wife, Sarah, looking through a photographer's prop of Queen Victoria and Prince Albert, 1992.

Brighton Rock, 1993. The origins of pink-lettered rock are a little obscure. Some of the early rock recorded in the 1850s had stripes and a little later confectioners experimented with designs of circles and flowers. It was not until the 1860 and 1870s that rock with girls' names first appeared, followed by the names of towns. No holiday in Brighton is complete without a stick of Brighton Rock; it is a quintessential part of our Britishness.

'The smallest art gallery in the world', July 1993, represents another interesting business use for the Old Chain Pier toll booth. Statistics supplied by the British Tourist Authority show that the Palace Pier had 3½ million visitors during 1997 and was one of the top ten attractions in the country.

The remodelled Palace of Fun, July 1993. Those who used the Palace Pier during the late 1960s recall the varied menu of amusements in the Palace of Fun. They were greeted at the entrance with the Mutoscopes, a relic of the early years. The other amusement machines were both mechanical and electrical, the former including one-armed bandits and the latter random flashing lights. The period also saw the rising popularity of pinball tables, first introduced from America in the 1920s. The air was filled with the sound of a distinctive clunking noise as the machines paid out the winners in old pennies. The central area was occupied by a popular bingo stall, operated by George Ticehurst and his assistant Gilbert, with prizes given to the lucky few.

Tattooing by Dave, including ear and nose piercing, 1994. A happy customer endures the pain of the pen. The practice of having indelible patterns punctured on to the skin has not diminished in popularity over the years. The word tattoo comes from Tahiti (tatau), which is the largest of the Society Islands in the South Pacific. Tahiti was visited by Captain James Cook in 1769 and by Bligh of the *Bounty* in 1788. Sailors copied the practice of tattooing from the local indigenous population.

Looking at the sea through the slats in the decking, July 1993. Children have always been fascinated but perhaps a little scared.

PALACE PIER

The children still look

Heavy metal turbo-coaster speakers
Drown out all talk that's sociable, fraternal,
Where once a band of Sussex Royal (Vols.)
Performed by kind permission of the colonel –
Yet the children still look.

Grotesque faces leer through holograms
To frighten souls within the spectrum den;
Where is Miss Amy Rayner's winning smile,
As 'Princess Charmante' of the Fair Glen?
Yet the children still look
Through the cracks in the boards.

Feeling low? Unbalanced? Press the screen!
Now palmistry prediction's automatic;
Who *was* 'The World's Greatest Equilibriste'?

Forget the stars, the past's more enigmatic –
And the children still look
Through the gaps in the boards
At the sea as it breaks.

Bored blonde in black awaits her plastic penguin,
As two men eye the target of their dreams;
If only she had seen the much admired Original
Anglo-American Bicycle Polo Team –
And the children still look
Through the gaps in the boards
At the sea as it breaks
Against pillars and struts.

Peter Brown, 9.2.97

Peter Brown lectures in English Literature at the University of Kent at Canterbury. He was a student at the University of Sussex, lived in Kemp Town, and remembers the Palace Pier with affection.

Balloon sellers at work on the forecourt of the busy Palace Pier, 1995. The fairground atmosphere is enhanced by music from the Casparini organ on this hot summer's day.

Its fame has spread far and wide. The Palace Pier, Brighton, in Miniland at LEGOLAND® Windsor. The model is made from 103,000 LEGO bricks and if the bricks were laid end to end, they would reach over three kilometres into the sea; seven times longer than the real pier. A caption near the model describes customers' reaction: 'it was almost like promenading on a fashionable cruise ship.'

Holidaymakers pose for the camera at the pier head, 1996.

Roller-coaster Turbo, 1998. This ride was installed on the pier during 1995. Upgrading of the pier's menu of attractions is a constant process, and 'fun-fair at sea' is an apt description of its modern incarnation.

Fish & Chips Cafe sign, Palace Pier, 1998. The first recorded reference to fried fish being sold from stalls was in London during the 1840s: 'One could buy a fillet of plaice or sole battered and fried in oil for 1*d*.' A slice of bread would be thrown in: chips and the deep pan fryer were not invented until the 1850s. The trade extended into coastal resorts, entering the very heart of seaside history.

All aboard the Carousel. This exquisite merry-go-round was introduced at the pier head in 1997. The design and painting of the horses demonstrate fine craftsmanship.

During March 1996 the pier was the setting for the launch of the Year of the Pier by the then Heritage Secretary, Virginia Bottomley. The Palace Pier was voted Pier of The Year in 1998 by the National Pier Society. We are sure these three youngsters would agree!

CHAPTER NINE

THE FUTURE

T he story of the forty-two piers around the British coast during the last thirty years has generally been one of neglect and decline. Many did not recover from the years of neglect and destruction during the Second World War, while others have been damaged by strong seas, collisions and fire. The fires at Southend-on-Sea's pier, the longest pier in the country, make national news but the list of destruction elsewhere is a long one. The West Pier at Brighton has been closed since 1975 and is a sorry ghost-like structure of rapidly peeling paint and rotting woodwork. Notices and barbed-wire warn the public to keep away.

Piers are notoriously difficult to destroy completely. They may be attacked by winter gales, high seas, shipping, fire and general neglect, but what remains is expensive to demolish, a task that local governments will often defer in the hope that future gales might save them the cost. Whatever remains tends to recall piers' former glory and brings into being organized groups dedicated to their restoration before they disappear for good. That revival of interest has led to the formation of the National Pier Society which attempts to coordinate interest and effort on a national scale, drawing upon local expertise and interests. The subject of piers encompasses a great deal of social, economic and local history, in addition to the development of art, engineering and shipping. It is not surprising, therefore, that the movement attracts people from many different walks of life.

In 1996 – The Year of the Pier – newspaper articles and radio and television programmes stimulated interest in the subject. This renewed concern for the structures' conservation, restoration or rebuilding possibly led to the announcement in 1997 that National Lottery money will be made available for some of the work. Brighton's West Pier, which needs an estimated £30 to £40 million spent upon it, has been promised assistance from the National Lottery, which makes it likely that the resort will soon be able to boast of two piers once again. Arguably some of the largest programmes, such as the complete rebuilding of Minehead Pier after nearly sixty years, are too ambitious; as an analogy, not even the keenest steam-railway enthusiast would expect the preservation of every engine and station from that past era, but would be satisfied with the restoration of some of the best representative examples.

In the absence of adequate funds, it is uncertain how other piers will survive. About half of them are run by trusts set up for that purpose while others are privately owned, including the Palace Pier which is in the hands of the Noble Organization. How the piers in the hands of the trusts will be treated in their applications for funding from the National Lottery has yet to be seen, and it may be a source of friction between them and the privately owned ones. This source of funding, however distributed, does demonstrate that the public is interested in their survival, whether privately owned or not. This allows us to be optimistic about the future of the Palace Pier which has shown in the past that it could adapt to changing public tastes and can doubtless do so again. If Brighton herself has a future as a resort, a proposition that few would deny, then the Palace Pier may remain a part of visitors' enjoyment by the sea for many years to come.

The lull before the storm as the pier prepares for another busy day. Photograph by John Hulme, c. 1990.

The Palace Pier from the east beach, c. 1997. The pier has played its part in reflecting the fascinating history of Brighton from its humble beginnings as a small fishing village to its current position as one of the UK's leading resorts.

ACKNOWLEDGEMENTS

We would like to thank the following organizations and individuals for their encouragement and the loan of and/or permission to use a number of photographs, postcards, drawings and paintings, which have greatly enriched this book:

The Noble Organization • The Royal Pavilion Libraries and Museums • *Evening Argus* (Newsquest Sussex Ltd) • Punch Ltd • Aerofilms Ltd • the Institute of Civil Engineers • Legoland Windsor • Victoria Art Gallery • Bath & North East Somerset • Professor David Welch • Professor David Birmingham • Dr Grayson Ditchfield • Dr Peter Brown • Jane Weeks • Daphne Leach • Jean Penny • Ronald Dalton • Peter Grilli • John Hulme • Andrew Barlow • Hilary Woodard • Roy Stevens • Silvia Walden • Marie White • Derek Whittaker • Trish Hatton • Monica and Dennis Holland • Maurice Hart • John Styles • Dorothy Crane • Mercia St Pourçain • Jenny Chapman • George Dobre • John Lloyd • L.V. Martin • John Haddaway • Jim Styles • David Peacock • Miranda Taylor • Janet Davidson • Penny Dalton • Ian Presland • Simon Anderson • James Gray • Philippe Garner.

Our special thanks go to William Everett who worked on the pier from 1947 to 1984, being General Manager from 1969. His precise recording of every detail has made our task that much easier. Dr John Whyman has placed his extensive knowledge on seaside history at our disposal and his criticisms and suggestions have been most valuable.

BRITAIN IN OLD PHOTOGRAPHS

SUTTON'S PHOTOGRAPHIC HISTORY OF TRANSPORT

To order any of these titles please telephone our distributor, Littlehampton Book Services on 01903 828800
For a catalogue of these and our other titles please ring Emma Leitch on 01453 731114